Climate Governance and Development

Climate Governance
and Development

Edited by
**Albrecht Ansohn
and Boris Pleskovic**

Internationale Weiterbildung   Capacity Building
und Entwicklung gGmbH   International, Germany

THE WORLD BANK
Washington, D.C.

ISBN: 978-0-8213-7994-3
eISBN: 978-0-8213-8307-0
DOI: 10.1596/978-0-8213-7994-3
ISSN: 1813-9442

Contents

ABOUT THIS BOOK   vii

INTRODUCTION   1
Aehyung Kim and Boris Pleskovic

OPENING ADDRESS   9
Carola Donner-Reichle

KEYNOTE ADDRESS
Climate Governance and Devlopment   11
Rosina Bierbaum

KEYNOTE ADDRESS
Development and Climate Change   27
Justin Yifu Lin

Part I   Climate Change as a Development Priority

Mainstreaming Climate Adaptation into Development: A Policy Dilemma   35
Richard J. T. Klein

Part II   Energy and Development: Policies and Technologies

Urbanization and Sustainable Cities: The Role of Governance, Infrastructure, and Technology   55
Judith A. Layzer

Promoting Research, Innovation, and Technology Transfers for Alternative Energy Sources   61
Claudia Kemfert

Part III Natural Resource Governance for Adaptation, Mitigation, and Development

Governance for Sustainable Adaptation? Environmental Stressors,
Natural Resources, and Human Security   71
Siri Eriksen

Impact of Climate and Land-Use Changes on Natural Resources in the
Agricultural Landscape   85
Andrzej Kędziora and Zbigniew W. Kundzewicz

Part IV Development, Non-State Actors, and Climate Governance: Private Sector and NGOs

Climate Change and the Threat to Development   107
David Rogers

Part V Financing Adaptation and Mitigation in an Unequal World

The International Climate Architecture and Financial Flows for Adaptation   121
Charlotte Streck

Part VI Changing Climate, Changing Institutions of Governance

Creating the Capacity for Decentralized, Self-Governing Adaptations
to Climate Change   133
John Scanlon and Clara Nobbe

The Politics of Climate Policy in Developed Countries   149
Hugh Compston and Ian Bailey

About This Book

The World Bank and InWEnt (Capacity Building International, Germany) hold a Development Policy Forum each September in Berlin. This meeting, known as the "Berlin Workshop," provides a forum for the European research community to contribute its perspectives to early discussions in preparation of the World Bank's annual *World Development Report*. The Workshop offers new ideas and distinctive perspectives from outside the World Bank. Participants in the Workshop come from a range of academic, governmental, think-tank, and policy-making institutions in Europe, the United States, and the Russian Federation, as well as from the World Bank and the German development institutions. Conference papers are written by the participants and are reviewed by the editors. Participants' affiliations identified in this volume are as of the time of the conference, September 28–30, 2008

The planning and organization for the 2008 workshop involved a joint effort. We extend our special thanks for the support of Justin Yifu Lin, senior vice president for development economics and chief economist of the World Bank, and Rosina Bierbaum and Marianne Fay, codirectors of the World Bank's *World Development Report 2010*. We wish to thank Aehyung Kim and Alexander Lotsch for their advice and suggestions. We would also like to thank the conference coordinators at InWEnt, Joachim Mueller and Katja Wehlte de Hernández, whose excellent organizational skills kept the workshop on track. Finally, we thank the editorial staff, especially Stuart Tucker and Mark Ingebretsen, from the Office of the Publisher.

Introduction

AEHYUNG KIM AND BORIS PLESKOVIC

This volume, Berlin Workshop Series 2010, contains a selection of papers presented at the 11th International Policy Workshop, held in Berlin, September 28–30, 2008. The workshop was jointly organized by Inwent–Capacity Building International, Germany, and the World Bank in preparation for the World Bank's *World Development Report 2010*. It provided a forum for an exchange of ideas and viewpoints that contributed to the development of the report.

Participants discussed development challenges and successes pertaining to climate change. Many poor and vulnerable communities and population groups are already bearing the burden of substantial climate impacts. Over time, such impacts are projected to become increasingly far-reaching, ubiquitous, and critical. In the six sessions of the workshop, participants explored the problems that climate change poses for development as they reflected on the challenges involved and discussed solutions to them.

In his keynote address, *Justin Lin* argues that climate change could be considered as the defining long-term development challenge of the 21st century. Unless we deal with climate change, other development challenges—poverty, inequality, demographic change, public health needs, natural catastrophes, and financial and terms-of-trade shocks, among others—will only become even more difficult to manage. Climate change threatens over time to reverse the development gains of recent years and limit prospects for further gains.

Lin describes the three objectives of the World Development Report. The first is to help convince the development community that climate change really does represent a changing environment for development, and that development "the way we've always done it" is no longer an effective option. The second is to build the case that unless development realities are fully integrated into agreements for

Aehyung Kim is a consultant, Development Economics at the World Bank. Boris Pleskovic is Research Manager, Development Economics at the World Bank.

Berlin Workshop Series 2010

mitigating greenhouse gases, such agreements will not deliver significant mitigation, or will simply fail. A third goal of the report is to contribute to the small but growing body of knowledge on how development policy should be designed in a "greenhouse world."

At the same time, Lin argues that two key challenges concern better management of energy sources and natural resources. How different sets of actors respond to these challenges will shape the future of a climate-stressed world, so the conference includes in-depth consideration of the strengths that different groups of actors can bring to the common goal of creating more effective responses to climate change. These include not only responses of policy, but also of the role that autonomous adaptation to climate change plays in complementing public sector actions or filling in when planned adaptations to climate change fall short.

In her opening address, *Rosina Bierbaum* states that an important part of the World Development Report is going to be to find solutions to climate change that are adequate, achievable and acceptable—the "triple A" response. Any of the versions of the "glowing ember" temperature charts indicate that today's temperatures are already beginning to have an impact. When the temperature reaches about 2 degrees C above preindustrial levels—roughly in the range of 450 parts per million—we will begin to see losses of food crops and significant decreases in water. These changes may impact perhaps 1 to 2 billion people and 20 to 40 percent of species, with many species threatened with extinction.

Bierbaum argues that it is becoming increasingly clear that the Millennium Development Goals (MDGs) are threatened by climate change. One must think about environmental sustainability and climate change all together in a context of multiple stressors. Climate change, says Bierbaum, touches all of the MDGs in ways that might make them unachievable. For instance, if crop yields decrease, the first goal is affected; if disease ranges shift, the fourth, fifth, and sixth goals are affected. If climate change affects intergenerational equity, we may be unable to achieve universal primary education or gender equality, or to empower women or to develop a global partnership for development. Clearly, if climate change is not addressed, nearly all of the Millennium Development Goals are at risk.

The World Development Report, Bierbaum states, will focus not only on how climate change affects development, but also on how development can and will affect climate change. If action to control greenhouse gases is delayed, the cost of achieving lower concentrations in the atmosphere will greatly increase. So the sooner all countries participate, the lower the total cost. But, of course, in order to have all countries participate, there would need to be massive monetary and technology flows from the North to the South.

Bierbaum also highlights that the World Development Report will integrate discussions of mitigation and adaptation, two concepts which are often not integrated. Chapters in Working Groups II and III of the Intergovernmental Panel on Climate Change (IPCC) tried to look at these. It is very important to understand how mitigation and adaptation might intersect. Some adaptations might interfere with steps taken toward mitigation. For example, if making biofuels viable is a mitigation goal, it might require quite a bit of water that otherwise would have been destined for adaptation activities involving fish or agriculture. If we fail to consider some of the intersections between mitigation and adaptation, we may miss important solution sets, or even identify sets that aren't really solutions.

At the same time, the WDR aims to present evidence that early action offers benefits for all countries, both in terms of economic costs to achieve a particular target and in societal benefits. The book will also highlight development opportunities in this changing competitive landscape. For example, countries that are blessed with sun might have a new resource to sell, or heavily forested countries could store carbon in their trees or their soils. It will be a different world. Past is no longer prologue.

Climate Change as a Development Priority

Part I looks at climate change as a challenge to development policy. *Richard J. T. Klein* argues for stronger efforts to support adaptation to climate change in developing countries. The potential to create synergies by integrating ("mainstreaming") adaptation into development activities is widely recognized, but in discussions on the financing of climate adaptation, proposals for such mainstreaming are viewed with suspicion. Developed countries have committed themselves to providing new and additional finance for adaptation in developing countries, but mainstreaming adaptation into development would make it more difficult to identify whether support for adaptation is indeed new and additional or represents, instead, a diversion of existing development finance. The author outlines this dilemma and calls on developed countries, in particular the European Union (EU) and its member states, to give priority to restoring mutual trust between developed and developing countries in the climate negotiations.

Energy and Development: Policies and Technologies

Part II highlights the role of technological innovation and alternative energy sources in promoting sustainable development. *Judith A. Layzer* discusses governance, infrastructure, and technology in the context of rapid urbanization and the construction of sustainable cities. The author argues that cities will be critical to the quest for sustainability in the twenty-first century. More than half the world's people live in cities. In developed countries, that figure is closer to three-quarters, and demographers predict that almost all population growth over the next 40 years is likely to occur in developing-country cities. Today's large cities became wealthy by overexploiting nonrenewable resources and by using remote places as sources of raw materials and as waste sinks. That path is no longer an option, for both economic and ecological reasons. The developing world will need an entirely new model of urban development—a trajectory based not on fossil fuels and export-driven economic growth but on integrated systems of local power generation, food production, water management, and waste reuse and recycling. Yet the global economy is currently based on ever-increasing, pollution-generating consumption, and many object that developing countries have more pressing priorities than sustainability. Local leadership that puts sustainability at the top of its agenda, bolstered by international funding for locally appropriate infrastructure and technology, will be an essential feature of governance in the world's emerging sustainable cities.

Claudia Kemfert notes that today's society faces two main energy-related threats: to guarantee a secure and affordable energy supply, and to reduce and eliminate environmental and climate damage caused by energy consumption. Over 80 percent of today's primary energy consumption comes from nonrenewable fossil fuels such as coal, oil, and natural gas. Without changes in behavior, the future share of fossil fuel resources in primary energy consumption will remain as high as it is today, leaving importing countries vulnerable to supply disruptions and energy price shocks. Furthermore, fossil fuel consumption generates greenhouse gas emissions, leading to climate change. As the International Energy Agency (IEA) argues, the future energy mix should not be underinvested, vulnerable, and dirty, but clean, clever, and competitive.

Kemfert states that secure, reliable, and affordable energy resources are fundamental to sustained economic development. The risk of disruptive climate change, the erosion of energy security, and the world's growing demand for energy all pose major challenges for energy decision makers. To meet these challenges and transform our energy system, a better use of existing technologies will be required, along with significant scientific innovation to spur the adoption of new energy technologies. Urgent action is needed to promote energy efficiency and low-carbon technologies and practices. Additional funding for basic science and energy research is critically needed to develop a sustainable energy future. Research priorities include photovoltaics, carbon capture and sequestration (CCS), biofuels, and hydrogen generation, storage, and use.

Natural Resource Governance for Adaptation, Mitigation, and Development

Part III examines natural resource governance. *Siri Eriksen* argues that governance for adaptation entails addressing existing power structures and the politics inherent in the adaptation process, in addition to strengthening institutional frameworks. Interventions or governance systems that focus on only one stressor or that assume homogeneity in a group can inadvertently increase exposure to stressors and reduce response capacity. Eriksen emphasizes that governance systems need to approach vulnerability and adaptation more holistically. This entails being able to grasp the diverse reasons for vulnerability within a heterogeneous group, even at a local level, and having the capacity and maneuvering space to develop cross-sectoral and sometimes "nonenvironmental" interventions. Putting adaptation and vulnerable groups first entails a reprioritization that has political ramifications and potentially involves challenging prevailing development discourses. Central issues include how institutions, rules, and regulations are set up to ensure various rights, such as labor rights, and whose interests are promoted in the operation of institutional and legal frameworks.

Building in principles of sustainable adaptation, with a focus on equity and environmental integrity, is one way of achieving governance for adaptation.

Andrzej Kędziora and *Zbigniew W. Kundzewicz* discuss the impact of climate and land-use changes on natural resources in the agricultural landscape. They argue that global climate conditions are created and determined mainly by three sets of factors: the physical processes and properties of the atmosphere, the chemical processes and composition of the atmosphere, and the properties of and processes at the Earth's surface. All three are influenced by human activity, and this has been especially true during the last century. Three processes—energy flows, cycling of matter, and global atmospheric circulation—are mainly responsible for the functioning of the climate system on different scales. The interaction between the atmosphere and the Earth's surface influences the effect of these three processes.

Agriculture will have to feed increasing human populations in the decades to come. Yet even now, many people suffer hunger or are undernourished, and it will be difficult to achieve the United Nations Millennium Development Goal (MDG) of halving, globally, the number of starving people by 2015. An essential task is to at least reverse the ongoing trends toward increased atmospheric concentrations of greenhouse gases and loss of vegetation, wetlands, and small water bodies. One of the best tools for managing the heat balance of the landscape is to plant shelterbelts, which reduce wind speed and conserve water.

Development, Nonstate Actors, and Climate Governance: The Private Sector and Nongovernmental Organizations

Part IV examines the role of the private sector and nongovernmental organizations in addressing climate change. *David Rogers* argues that climate change threatens to reduce or even reverse the gains made toward sustainable development. Countries are wrestling with the need to mitigate climate impacts in the long term, but adaptation offers the only way of coping with the inevitable effects of climate change over the next few decades. Developing economies are particularly vulnerable; not only are they predominantly poor and exposed to natural hazards, but many lack the capacity to provide climate risk information to their own citizens or to manage disaster risk effectively, and few possess dedicated climate services. Rogers describes the emerging role of national meteorological and hydrological services (NMHSs) in developing countries and examines some issues surrounding their activities.

Mainstreaming the reduction of climate change risks into development is a priority that requires the translation of existing international commitments into action. Support by the international community for construction of national monitoring and dissemination programs must be accompanied by institution building aimed at enabling governments to incorporate climate information into economic development programs. Collaboration by a wide range of stakeholders is needed to promote understanding of and response to the implications of climate change for disaster risk and development. A holistic approach requires the integration of social, economic, and environmental information to permit full understanding of the impact of climate on development and to inform policy decisions in all the interconnected sectors—health, energy, agriculture, urban development, and so on.

Financing Adaptation and Mitigation in an Unequal World

Part V explores financing mechanisms for climate change mitigation and adaptation. *Charlotte Streck* argues that climate change affects livelihoods, food security, and the economic output of developing countries. Among the expected effects of climate change are increased water scarcity and declining water quality, warming and acidification of the world's oceans, sea-level rise and the associated coastal impacts, extreme weather events, climate-related impacts on public health, and additional threats to forest ecosystems and endangered species. With changes in the climate becoming more prominent every year, adaptation is no longer just another policy option. Robust adaptation strategies to increase the climate resilience of local livelihoods and the domestic economy form an essential part of the international response to climate change. Developing countries, however, often lack the means, technology, and institutional capacity to adapt effectively to changing climatic conditions and increased risks of extreme weather. These countries will need international support, as well as stable and predictable funding to formulate policies and to build and establish national capacities. Streck proposes that adaptation efforts in developing countries be supported by multiple sources, including funds mandated by the United Nations Framework Convention on Climate Change (UNFCCC) and bilateral resources. Developed-country contributions to those funds should be complemented by new forms of funding, such as a share of proceeds on carbon market transactions, a fee on bunker fuels, or other financing mechanisms. Since market-based mechanisms such as carbon trading are unlikely to support adaptation finance, it will be more difficult to attract private funding and investment into adaptation than into mitigation measures. Adaptation therefore needs to become an integrated part of a country's general development policy, backed by official development assistance (ODA) and by national, multilateral, and dedicated climate funds supporting developing countries' transition toward climate-resilient economies.

Changing Climate, Changing Institutions of Governance

Part VI addresses the capacity and governance of developing countries in mitigating climate change. *John Scanlon* and *Clara Nobbe* discuss the creation of capacity for decentralized, self-governing adaptation to climate change. The authors cite the finding of the Fourth Assessment Report of the IPCC, that adaptation has become as important a response to climate change as mitigation. In fact, failure to take effective adaptive measures will threaten the achievement of most of the MDGs and will have severe implications for the well-being of populations in both developing and developed countries. Following an outline of the water-related impacts of climate change, which will disproportionately affect disadvantaged groups in developing countries, Scanlon and Nobbe investigate the main adaptation needs: governance and institutional requirements, additional investments, greater collaboration between the science community and policy makers; and technological development. They acknowledge the challenges associated with effective adaptation but also see opportunities for tackling the adaptation challenge by integrating adaptive measures into existing governance systems. Effective adaptation, they conclude. requires greater emphasis on local solutions, including the strengthening of local governance structures.

Hugh Compston and *Ian Bailey* report on a study of the politics of climate policy, in affluent democracies and at the EU level, that aimed at identifying political strategies which may enable governments to make major cuts in greenhouse gas emissions without sustaining significant political damage (Compston and Bailey 2008). Although the study focused on developed countries, many of its findings are relevant to developing countries. Compston and Bailey analyze six major obstacles to the implementation of more radical climate policies: the perception that actions by individual countries make little difference; the continued influence of climate skeptics; a shortage of technically and economically efficacious solutions; the problem of competitiveness; fear of the electorate; and obstacles within government. They then outline the main political strategies currently being used by governments in the countries reviewed in the study to strengthen climate policy: (a) striving to reach global agreement on policies to control climate change; (b) commissioning reports and setting targets; (c) implementing climate policies on which all major relevant political actors can agree; (d) implementing incremental policy changes; (e) taking advantage of weather-related natural disasters to heighten awareness of climate risks; (f) framing climate policies as contributing to other desired policy objectives; and (g) choosing appropriate policy instruments, which may include information provision, technological fixes, renewable energy, energy efficiency, voluntary agreements, emissions trading, and carbon and energy taxes. The authors draw some tentative conclusions about the applicability of their findings for developing countries. It is noted that all the identified obstacles apply to developing countries (although authoritarian regimes may be able to be bolder than democratic governments) and that lack of resources constitute an additional obstacle for the developing group. The political strategies identified are also germane, although in some countries the extent of political polarization may make agreement on climate policies difficult, if not impossible.

Reference

Compston, Hugh, and Ian Bailey, eds. 2008. *Turning Down the Heat: The Politics of Climate Policy in Affluent Democracies.* Houndmills, Basingstoke, Hampshire, U.K.: Palgrave Macmillan.

Opening Address

CAROLA DONNER-REICHLE

Dear Rosina Bierbaum, Justin Yifu Lin, and participants,

Welcome to Berlin and to our International Policy Workshop, which takes place each year in preparation for the World Bank's *World Development Report*.

The Fourth Assessment Report of the Intergovernmental Panel on Climate Change (IPCC) made observations on the first effects of climate change. The impacts of climate change will be experienced by many groups in society and across many economic sectors. They will include flood risk, reduced biodiversity, food insecurity, economic production losses, and increased health risks. There is no way to address the resulting problems effectively—whether by reducing greenhouse gas emissions or by protecting habitat vital to threatened or endangered species—without changing human behavior, both individual and collective. Climate change is not an environmental challenge; it is a development challenge for our time.

Global action on climate change will require global cooperation and global governance. For the United Nations conference on climate change in Copenhagen in December 2009, North and South will have to work together to meet this challenge. Policy makers at all levels need better knowledge of the demographic, economic, social, institutional, and technological problems that lead to increases in greenhouse gas emissions and the destruction of the ecosystem. We also need a response on a global level. All these challenges require new and innovative forms of governance.

As noted by the United Nations University's Institute for Environment and Human Security, several studies have dealt with global environmental governance. Two traditional forms of government have dominated world affairs until recently: national governments working through governmental regulations, and international government decisions for collective action facilitated by international organizations and international regimes. Sustainable development requires an understanding that actions have

Carola Donner-Reichle is director of the Social Development Department at InWEent–Capacity Building International, Germany.

Berlin Workshop Series 2010

consequences and that humanity must find innovative ways of changing institutional structures and influencing individual behavior. Accordingly, our policy workshop discusses how to link those insights on climate and development, with emphasis on the question of climate governance.

A new catchword in the draft *World Development Report* drew my attention: "climate smart." What does this mean? Yesterday, I saw a feature on television about how wine growers in my home area of Baden-Württemberg, Germany, are adjusting to climate change by planting different types of grapes. That is smart!

I would like to introduce InWEnt–Capacity Building International, which organized this conference on behalf of the Federal Ministry of Economic Cooperation and Development. InWEnt—Internationale Weiterbildung und Entwicklung gGmbH—is an implementing organization of the German government that promotes international human resource development, advanced training, and dialogue, thus making an integral and targeted contribution to international cooperation by building structures for sustainable development. "Program-focused capacity building" is a goal-oriented investment in human potential. Our political mission is to focus on the practice-oriented advanced training of experts and executives, fostering, predominantly, operative performing and functional elites but also up-and-coming decision makers in politics, administration, the private sector, and civil society. Inwent offers political decision makers networks that, through exchange of experience, enable them to carry out reform and change processes. Its key tasks include facilitating access to innovative knowledge, providing a platform for exchange of experience, and offering advanced training programs for managers. Our overall goal is to strengthen the skills of decision makers in political, organizational, and private sector change processes.

Finally, I would like to say something about this venue. The Mövenpick Hotel, where we meet today, is a historic place. It was originally the Siemens House, built in 1914 by the Siemens Company to give the firm a permanent address in the center of Berlin. The room we are in, the Siemens Saal, survived the destructive forces of World War II and the isolation imposed by the Berlin Wall, which stood nearby. We are in the middle, between East and West Berlin. When Berlin assumed its old role as the capital of Germany some years ago, the Siemens House drew attention because it is a singular witness to what this quarter once was and because of its roots in the Siemens Company.

At the beginning of the twentieth century, Siemens was producing all those things that imparted a new pace to urban life: a suburban railway, streetcars, traffic lights, telephones, and street lighting. Siemens made a huge contribution toward making Berlin the capital of electricity, an electropolis, so to speak. This spirit of innovation will guide our endeavors during the next two days as we think about and discuss solutions to the challenge of climate governance and development that we face. I am convinced that the proceedings of the workshop will be an important input in drafting *World Development Report 2010*. I wish us all inspiring days in Berlin, and I hope you enjoy your stay here. Thank you very much!

Keynote Address
Climate Governance and Development

ROSINA BIERBAUM

It is wonderful to have so many wise friends here to help us think about *World Development Report 2010.* I believe that our conference—the latest in a series of meetings held each year to prepare for the *World Development Report (WDR)*—will be very exciting. I want to thank Capacity Building International (InWEnt) and the German Federal Ministry for Economic Cooperation and Development for arranging this event.

The Report is called the *"World" Development Report,* so its scope is worldwide, but it is also the *World "Development" Report,* which means there has to be a focus on development. The *WDR* is always about development and "something." This year, for the first time, the topic is development and climate change. Creating a unique value added will be tricky in this very busy world of climate reports. We see virtually one such report every week—in fact, probably one a week from every country. I am looking forward to your wisdom in helping us sort through all the possible topics that this *WDR* might cover and how we can bring governance to bear in the Report in a unique way.

During the conference, you will hear from many *WDR* team members, but I will point them out now. Justin Lin is the chief economist of the World Bank, and Marianne Fay is *WDR* codirector, along with me. (I am the scientist, and she is the economist.) A number of team members are here, as well: Arun Agrawal, Andrea Liverani, Alex Lotsch, and Ian Noble. Later, two of our academic advisers, Nebojsa Nakicenovic and John Schellnhuber, will join us.

I know I am standing between you and dinner. So let me try to be a bit provocative to get our evening conversations going. Tomorrow, Justin Lin will "refocus" us regarding the task at hand and how this particular conference fits into the *WDR.*

Rosina Bierbaum is the codirector of *World Development Report 2010.*
Berlin Workshop Series 2010
© 2010 The International Bank for Reconstruction and Development / The World Bank

Keep in mind, as we think about how best to position this Report, that it will be on the streets by this time next year, in 2009, and will be pretty much public by late summer of next year. With all of the Copenhagen negotiations swirling around, we want to be helpful to that process, not inhibitory to it.

An exciting thing about this conference is that everybody in this room recognizes that climate change is a serious problem and that we should get on with addressing it. With the different disciplines represented here, I think we can start to develop a much-needed plan, a "how to" for addressing climate change. What is the strategy for getting from where society is today to where we think it needs to be in about 2030 if we are to stabilize atmospheric concentrations of greenhouse gases? Many reports end by saying that there is a problem and offer a laundry list of all the possible things that can be done for mitigation or for adaptation in all possible sectors. The result is a menu of ideas, but no substantive way to turn them into a strategy.

Principal Messages and Issues

Let me start with how we see our Report: as a call to action. We will clearly state that although climate change is one among many challenges facing developing countries, it is a very important challenge. Unless it is tackled soon, it will reverse the progress that has been made in development and can actually exacerbate inequalities. We will call for "climate-smart development" and will argue that it can be achieved. This is not development as it has been traditionally known, because the past is not a good surrogate for the future, and many things must be done a little differently. The only way to solve the problem of climate change is for the rich countries to take leadership on climate action now. But the atmosphere cannot be stabilized unless the very fast-growing countries also cooperate. So, the *WDR* starts with these messages in our call to action. You all know, of course, that the ecological and societal effects of climate change are much less well understood than the physical and chemical aspects. What must be done is to figure out how the impacts on human resources, natural resources, and infrastructure can be altered or controlled—in both anticipatory and reactive modes, but, preferably, more anticipatory.

It was exciting that at the recent Nobel Peace Prize event in Oslo, when Al Gore and the International Panel on Climate Change (IPCC) shared the award, all the scientists who made up the delegation from the IPCC's Working Group I agreed that the science is unequivocal. But it took 20 years to get to that point. I would argue that research in the field of adaptation now lags by at least 10 years, and if you believe most of the scientists, only 10 years remain in which to begin to turn this "supertanker" of global emissions around in order to prevent "dangerous anthropogenic interference with the climate systems."[1] We have to move a little faster on getting to solution sets.

FIGURE 1.
A Village on the Edge: Bangladesh

Source: Gary Braasch, World View of Global Warming, http://www.worldviewofglobalwarming.org.

Economic, Ecological, and Social Vulnerability

Of course, it is not just the aggregate impacts that determine how climate change affects you; it is also where you live. Figure 1 illustrates that for particular people in particular parts of the world, climate change will mean irreversible changes to their lifestyles. It is necessary to understand the ecological and socioeconomic impacts—how they affect people in particular regions, and what can be done about these effects. Societies' ability to cope will depend on the scientific, technological, and economic resources that can be brought to bear in different parts of the globe.

William Cline suggests that, looking at temperature only and without accounting for water, some parts of the world (the darker portions of figure 2) will experience declines in agricultural productivity of perhaps as much as 50 percent. These areas are the poorest countries of the world, which are already subject to poverty and famine. Schellnhuber (in SEG 2007) has examined this effect in a slightly different

FIGURE 2.
Farming in a Warmer World: Change in Crop Yield Potential by 2080

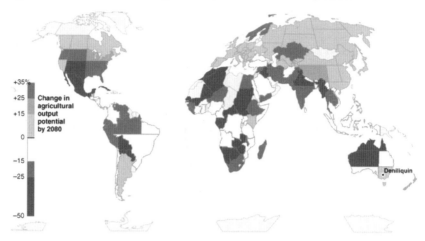

Source: Cline 2007.

Note: Crop forecasts indicate that some countries farther from the Equator could benefit from a warmer world, but others would be worse off by 2080 if global warming were to proceed unchecked. Long-range forecasts vary widely; the map represents a synthesis of available forecasts by country or region. The figures assume that crops grow faster because of higher levels of carbon dioxide in the air. Some scientists, however, believe that the actual effects of global warming could be worse than shown here because the benefits of extra carbon dioxide may not materialize if crops lack proper rainfall, proper soil, and clean air.

way, looking at agroeconomic vulnerability (figure 3). Again, the darker colors identify the more vulnerable countries. If more than 5 percent of a country's gross domestic product (GDP) comes from agriculture and the country loses one major crop, that is considered high vulnerability. Again, the analysis indicates that the impacts will be disproportionally felt by the poorest countries.

An important part of the *WDR* is going to be finding solutions to climate change that are adequate, achievable, and acceptable—the "triple A" response. Temperature charts such as figure 4, from the Stern Review (Stern 2007), indicate that at today's temperatures, designated by the heavy solid line, impacts are already beginning to be felt. By about 2°C above preindustrial levels, which is roughly the 450 parts per million (ppm) range, we will begin to see losses of food crops and significant decreases in water. These changes will affect perhaps 1 billion to 2 billion people and perhaps 20 to 40 percent of species; many species will be threatened with extinction. The precautionary principle that is built into the United Nations Framework Convention on Climate Change (UNFCCC) suggests that we should strive to stay out of the range of 3°C (approximately 550 ppm) and beyond. The more that is learned about the details—what might be called the "devil in the details"—of climate change, the greater is the realization that there are surprises that do not seem to be happening in ways that make us more sanguine. Those unpleasant surprises include nonlinearities or tipping points (whether small or large), some of which are already occurring or

FIGURE 3.
Agroeconomic Vulnerability to Future Climate Change: Effects on Gross Domestic Product (GDP) of Change in Agricultural Production, 2061–70

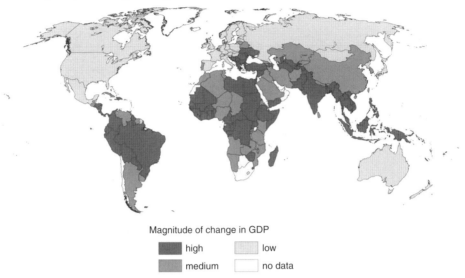

Magnitude of change in GDP

high   low
medium   no data

Source: SEG 2007.

Note: See SEG (2007) for assumptions and sources. "High" vulnerability denotes a significant yield loss in at least one important crop in a country where the share of agriculture in GDP is greater than 5 percent. "Low" vulnerability denotes low dependency on agriculture and a decrease in only one significant crop yield, or no decrease at all. The two remaining combinations are designated "medium."

FIGURE 4.
Effects of Global Temperature Change

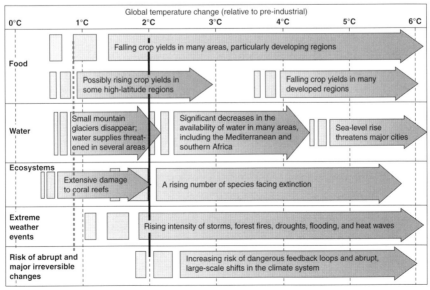

Source: Stern 2007.

are anticipated. For example, in the southwestern United States, a drought that was not particularly of record intensity, with a 1°C rise in temperature, led to massive pest infestations and significant tree die-offs from the combination of heat stress and drought. The unexpected rapid melting of the Arctic Sea ice and of the huge Greenland ice sheet cannot be accounted for in current models, and recent reports of methane chimneys in Siberia have raised fears that the permafrost "lid" may be thawing and leading to a runaway feedback effect.

According to the IPCC (IPCC 2007), datasets covering 20,000 species indicate that species are already on the move, shifting an average of 6 meters altitudinally, or 6 kilometers toward the poles, every decade. Speaking as an ecologist, these rates of change are worrisome because they exceed those occurring naturally on the planet in the last 10,000 years, during which time human beings domesticated animals and developed agricultural practices. Many might argue that in terms of the triple-A criteria, a goal of limiting temperature increases to a range of 2–2.5° C above preindustrial levels would be adequate. That view, however, ignores the questions of what is achievable, what is acceptable, and how the goal is to be achieved. I hope that we can focus on the second and third "A's" at this meeting.

I think many of us agree that climate change could become the biggest environmental injustice of all. It certainly can worsen current inequities, as the impacts of climate change continue to fall on the poorest of the world, who have the least resources, whether scientific, technological, or economic, with which to respond. But climate change also threatens equity across regions, across time, and, potentially, across generations, as several participants in this conference have written.

Threats to the Millennium Development Goals

It is becoming increasingly clear that the Millennium Development Goals (MDGs) are threatened by climate change. (Box 1 contains a brief summary of the goals and their targets.) The seventh goal, that of ensuring environmental sustainability, is complicated because climate change is already interacting with air and water pollution, accelerating the decline in species diversity, the spread of invasive species, and habitat loss and fragmentation. One must think about environmental sustainability and climate change together, in a multiple-stress context. I would argue that climate change touches all the other Millennium Development Goals, in ways that might make them unachievable. If crop yields decrease, the first goal, that of ending poverty and hunger, is jeopardized; if disease ranges shift, that affects the fourth, fifth, and sixth goals, which concern health. If we are, in fact, endangering intergenerational equity, we may be unable to achieve universal primary education or gender equality, or to empower women, or to develop a Global Partnership for Development (the second, third, and eighth goals). Clearly, if climate change is not addressed, virtually all the Millennium Development Goals are at risk.

Challenges of Mitigating Climate Change

I mentioned that the precautionary principle was built into the UNFCCC. As an underlying thesis of our Report, we are not just thinking about discount rates (although many economists are working on that facet) but are, rather, taking the position that the precautionary principle should apply because of the risks of irreversibility, tipping points, and unsustainable development. Even if the world constrains greenhouse gas concentration in the atmosphere to 450 ppm, we have only

---

Box 1. The Eight Millennium Development Goals and Their Targets

Goal 1. Eradicate extreme poverty and hunger.
- Halve, between 1990 and 2015, the proportion of people whose income is less than US$1 a day.
- Achieve full and productive employment and decent work for all, including women and young people.
- Halve, between 1990 and 2015, the proportion of people who suffer from hunger.

Goal 2. Achieve universal primary education.
- Ensure that, by 2015, children everywhere, boys and girls alike, will be able to complete a full course of primary schooling.

Goal 3. Promote gender equality and empower women.
- Eliminate gender disparity in primary and secondary education, preferably by 2005, and at all levels of education no later than 2015.

Goal 4. Reduce child mortality.
- Reduce by two-thirds, between 1990 and 2015, the under-five mortality rate.

Goal 5. Improve maternal health.
- Reduce by three-quarters, between 1990 and 2015, the maternal mortality ratio.
- Achieve universal access to reproductive health.

Goal 6. Combat HIV/AIDS, malaria, and other diseases.
- Have halted by 2015 and begun to reverse the spread of HIV/AIDS.
- Achieve, by 2010, universal access to treatment for HIV/AIDS for all those who need it.
- Have halted by 2015 and begun to reverse the incidence of malaria and other major diseases.

(continued)

Box 1. The Eight Millennium Development Goals and Their Targets (*continued*)

Goal 7. Ensure environmental sustainability.
- Integrate the principles of sustainable development into country policies and programs and reverse the losses of environmental resources.
- Reduce biodiversity loss, achieving, by 2010, a significant reduction in the rate of loss.
- Halve, by 2015, the proportion of people without sustainable access to safe drinking water and basic sanitation.
- By 2020, to have achieved a significant improvement in the lives of at least 100 million slum dwellers.

Goal 8. Develop a Global Partnership for Development.
- Address the special needs of the least developed countries, landlocked countries, and small island developing states.
- Develop further an open, rule-based, predictable, nondiscriminatory trading and financial system.
- Deal comprehensively with developing countries' debt.
- In cooperation with pharmaceutical companies, provide access to affordable essential drugs in developing countries.
- In cooperation with the private sector, make available the benefits of new technologies, especially information and communications.

Source: United Nations, "We Can End Poverty—2015 Millennium Development Goals." http://www.un.org/millenniumgoals/.

---

a 50 percent chance of stopping at 2°C above preindustrial temperatures. The effort to understand and limit impacts on human beings and on ecosystems must be very concerted and must begin very soon. Carol Browner, the former head of the U.S. Environmental Protection Agency (EPA), has said that our generation has the capability of becoming the first to leave the next generation a truly irreversible problem—certainly, a moniker we do not want.

Why is climate change a serious development issue? Figure 5 presents estimates of the number of people affected by climate-related disasters—floods, droughts, hurricanes, and so on. People in developing countries are affected at 20 times the rate of those in developed countries, and, as you can see from the figure, these trends are likely to continue. The *WDR* will focus not only on how climate affects development but also on how development patterns will affect climate change. In the past, the rich countries were responsible for putting most of the greenhouse gases into the atmosphere, but that is going to change in the future. If action to control greenhouse gases is delayed, the cost of achieving any particular concentration in the atmosphere greatly increases. So, the sooner all countries participate, the lower will be the total cost. But in order to have all countries participate, massive monetary and technology flows from the North to the South are needed.

FIGURE 5.
Populations Affected by Climate-Related Disasters, by Decade

Source: World Bank analysis based on data from the Centre for Rural Education and Development (CREDA).

FIGURE 6.
Fossil Fuel Carbon Emissions: Historical Emissions, 1850–2005 and Scenarios to 2300

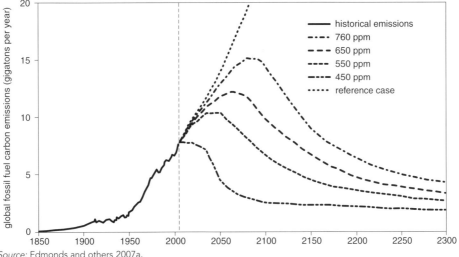

Source: Edmonds and others 2007a.

Note: ppm, parts per million. Estimates are from the Global Energy Technology Strategy Program (GTSP). By 2100, total carbon in the atmosphere, according to the various scenarios, are as follows: reference case, 1,430 gigatons; 750 ppm, 1,200 gigatons; 650 ppm, 1,040 gigatons; 550 ppm, 862 gigatons; 450 ppm, 480 gigatons.

If you look at the "business as usual" path and then at the 550 ppm line, at 10 billion tons of carbon (figure 6), with about 10 billion people in the world, that would be a ton of carbon per person. Multiplying that by 3.66 yields close to 4 tons of carbon dioxide per person. The United States, and most of the

FIGURE 7.
Carbon Dioxide Emissions by Country, 2002

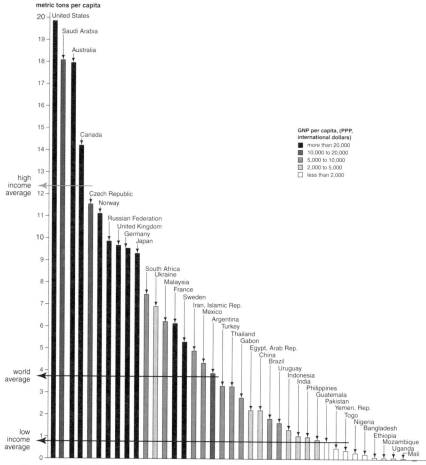

Source: Data from UNDP 2007.

Note: GNP, gross national product; PPP, purchasing power parity.

wealthy countries, would have to reduce their emissions about 80 percent to allow the world to get on a sustainable trajectory, which peaks just about now for 450 ppm and very soon for 550 ppm.

Of course, equity is crucial to all the negotiations. The United States now emits 20 metric tons of carbon dioxide per capita (figure 7). Germany is at about 10 tons per capita, and the average for low-income countries is about 1 ton. (Some countries, such as Nigeria and Bangladesh, are at very low levels.) These figures have changed slightly in the four years since the estimates were made, but the issues of ethics, of equity, and of building partnerships to deal with the problems of the "atmospheric commons" remain large. As we move toward Copenhagen, it is clear that for developing countries, it is either a "fair deal" or "no deal." And figuring out what "fair" entails is very important.

An Integrative Approach

What can *World Development Report 2010* contribute in this complex milieu, in which much research remains to be done—a lot of economic analysis, evaluation of many interactions, and the identification of realistic options? The *WDR*'s unique value added is, of course, its focus on development. The *Human Development Report* (UNDP 2007) had a focus on development, as have some other reports, but few climate reports bring out the issues of the poorest countries of the world. These countries do not now make much difference to emissions, but as they develop, it will be possible to put in place either good or bad energy systems that will facilitate or impede the use and preservation of their natural resource space.

The *WDR* team is determined that the Report will integrate discussions of mitigation and adaptation, which is not often done. (The reports of IPCC Working Groups II and III did contain chapters that looked at these issues.) There are a number of intersections that are important to understand. Some actions aimed at adaptation might interfere with mitigation activities. For example, if biofuels are embraced as a mitigation activity, quite a bit of water that otherwise might have been destined for fish or people or agriculture might be needed to make them viable. By failing to consider the intersections of mitigation and adaptation, we are missing important solution sets, or even identifying sets that are not really solutions.

The Case for Early Action

We want to present evidence that the elements of an international deal exist and to show why it is in everyone's best interest to act earlier rather than later. Why would there be enormous deadweight losses if action were not taken early on? If accession by developing countries were delayed by 40 years, some greenhouse gas concentration goals, such as the 450 ppm goal, could not be achieved, and the costs for other targets would also increase. We are hoping to present evidence that early action offers benefits for all countries—both in terms of economic costs to achieve a particular target, and in societal benefits. We also want to highlight development opportunities in this changing competitive landscape. Countries that are blessed with sunlight might have a new resource to sell; heavily forested countries could store carbon in their trees or in their soils. It will be a different world. The past is no longer prologue. The competitive landscape is not going to be the same as it has historically been, either.

Structure of the Report

Here is our proposed outline for the *WDR* (see box 2). Part 1 will discuss development policy that is informed by the concerns of climate change. Such "climate-smart" development policy will consider land and water challenges together. Many past analyses were conducted sectorally, with no provision for ensuring enough land and water for everything—agriculture, forests, cities, people, and wildlife.

Water may be the linchpin of climate change. Figure 8 shows the areas where water is scarce because of pricing and the areas where it is physically scarce or is

Box 2. Outline of World Development Report 2010

Part 1. Climate-smart development policy
- The land and water challenge: Managing competing demands and creating new opportunities
- The energy challenges: Managing competing objectives and creating a new comparative advantage
- Managing human vulnerability: Helping people help themselves

Part 2. Development-smart climate policy
- An international architecture for climate change and development
- Harnessing finance and market instruments for mitigation and adaptation
- Harnessing innovation and technology diffusion for mitigation and adaptation

Part 3. Achieving climate-smart decisions
- Global problems, local action; effective national and community-level actions
- Getting to decisions: Managing the politics and social psychology of climate change
- Getting to *good* decisions: Institutions and information; adaptive policies and governance

FIGURE 8.
Areas of Physical and Economic Water Shortage

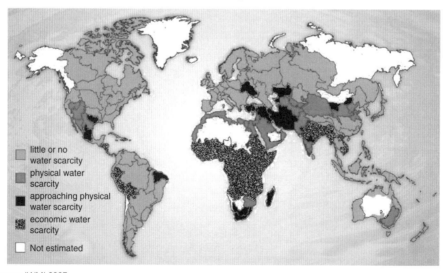

- little or no water scarcity
- physical water scarcity
- approaching physical water scarcity
- economic water scarcity
- Not estimated

Source: IWMI 2007.

approaching physical scarcity. If this water map were overlaid on areas of political instability, that would identify yet another layer of problems that affect a significant portion of the world. An overlay detailing how climate change is likely to change the availability of water in different seasons and the quality of water would add another set of problems that would exacerbate the situation.

Part 1 will also discuss the challenges of managing competing objectives to increase needed energy services for the world's population and to decrease greenhouse gas emissions significantly. It will include evaluations of how to manage human vulnerability, to help people help themselves. The United Nations High Commissioner for Refugees estimates that by 2030, there will be 30 million environmental refugees, even without climate change, and climate change will likely bump up that number by several tens of millions (SEG 2007, box 3.3). How can we empower people, from the local level to the national level, and build institutions so that people can help themselves in responding not only to extreme events but also to changing averages and a changing baseline—representing not just a response shift but a cultural one as well?

A land-use scenario issued by the Pacific Northwest National Laboratory in 2007 (Edmonds and others 2007b) shows that if the world attempts to reduce carbon dioxide emissions by growing a swath of biomass to replace fossil fuels, there could be detrimental effects on biodiversity unless we also value the carbon in trees and forests. In the absence of such assignment of value, the land needed for biofuels will likely come from unmanaged landscapes. Understanding of the interactions of activities that may be implemented to respond to climate change, and the composite consequences for land and water, biodiversity, energy, and people, is very important. Such integrative analyses are nascent efforts at this point.

Part 2 will examine "development-smart climate policy"—climate policy that takes into account what developing countries need. We want to talk about what the elements of a fair deal might be and to provide information about how the timing and stringency of agreements involving different countries would affect the atmosphere. Also to be examined is the harnessing of finance and market instruments for mitigation and adaptation. Much more money is needed to seriously tackle both sides of the climate problem. Innovation must be expedited in order to develop the next generation of technology and foster enhanced diffusion of best practices for both mitigation and adaptation. Understanding of innovation in adaptation is currently limited, and research must be accelerated. The all-time high in public research and development (R&D) was about US$11 billion per year; it is now about US$8 billion. Private energy R&D is also only in the tens of billions of dollars. Yet there are hundreds of billions of dollars of energy supply technologies that need to be deployed in developing countries, and quickly. The expenditure is simply incommensurate with the task.

In terms of innovation, the size of the challenge is clear when one looks at the amount of carbon capture and sequestration (CCS) needed to produce a significant effect in keeping atmospheric concentrations from exceeding 550 ppm. As figure 9 shows, by 2020, 70 times as much carbon would need to be stored as is

FIGURE 9.
Carbon Storage Requirements for Maintaining Atmospheric Concentration of Carbon Dioxide of 550 ppm or Less

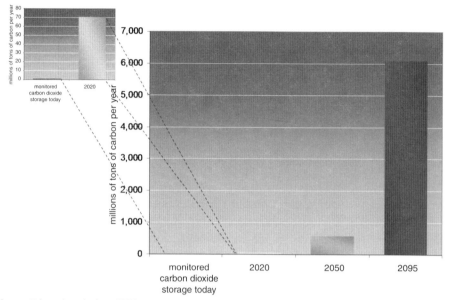

Source: Edmonds and others 2007a.

sequestered in geologic reserves today (about a million tons at present). By 2050, the scale would rise to 600 times today's level, and by 2100 the world would need to be storing 6 *billion* tons of carbon. How many demonstration plants will be needed, where can they be placed, what size should they be, and how fast can they be demonstrated, proved, and deployed?

Adaptation can occur in human systems or in natural systems, and it can be anticipatory or reactive. Anticipatory is certainly preferable. There are clearly categories of things that can be done on the human, socioeconomic plane, such as changing farming practices, developing early-warning systems, and so on. To date, however, most analysts have not come up with ideas for helping natural systems prepare for climate change. I think we must develop anticipatory actions for natural systems. In light of the prospect of losing 20 to 40 percent of the world's species at 2–2.5°C above preindustrial levels, it becomes crucial that we evaluate ways to enhance the resiliency and flexibility of these natural systems, or they may not persist. I would argue that there is a big research effort into adaptation that is currently missing. The *WDR* will discuss the moneys available for adaptation, but these are small and are scattered across many different funds.

Part 3 will focus on how to get to a climate-smart world. How do you mix and match all the tools in your toolkit to achieve climate-smart decisions? It is a global problem, but local action is needed, on the politics, the psychology, the finance, and the institutions. The *WDR* should serve as a road map to climate-smart decisions.

The *WDR* team is very interested in your feedback on the storyline and the key messages. We are also interested in your views on the framing. Should we emphasize

FIGURE 10.
The Earth at Night: 2000

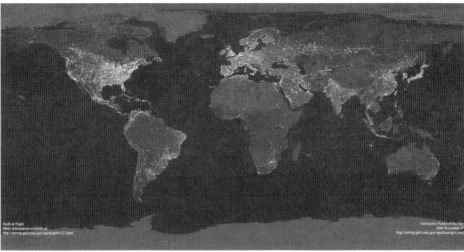

Source: U.S. National Aeronautics and Space Administration (NASA), "Astronomy Picture of the Day," November 27, 2000. http://hdr.undp.org/en/media/HDR_20072008_EN_Complete.pdf.

the urgency of the situation and the dire outcomes that are projected? Or should we be focusing more on the vision and opportunity that a world of green technologies and rapid innovation offers? What is the correct balance? There certainly are opportunities for reduced emissions, deforestation, and degradation (REDD). What should we be saying about bottom-up adaptation approaches versus top-down incentives? Case studies will be liberally strewn throughout the Report. We welcome studies of good and bad cases, examples of good adaptation, examples of maladaptation, and, in particular, examples of how to design an adequate, acceptable, and achievable response to the climate challenge.

I want to end with one of Marianne Fay's favorite graphics, a "lights at night" shot of the Earth (figure 10). It is quite amazing to see how many parts of the world are still dark. How we light those parts of the world, and with what kinds of energy, will determine whether we do leave the next generation with a truly irreversible problem or whether we have helped achieve a sustainable planet and a level of carbon dioxide that is acceptable to all the world's citizens.

Thank you for your attention.

References

Cline, William A. 2007. *Global Warming and Agriculture: Impact Estimates by Country.* Washington, DC: Peterson Institute for International Economics.

Edmonds, J., M. A. Wise, J. J. Dooley, S. H. Kim, S. J. Smith, P. J. Runci, L. E. Clarke, E. L. Malone, and G. M. Stokes. 2007a. "Global Energy Technology Strategy: Addressing Climate Change. Phase 2 Findings from an International Public-Private Sponsored Research

Program." Joint Global Change Research Institute, College Park, MD. http://www.globalchange.umd.edu/data/gtsp/docs/gtsp_2007_final.pdf.

Edmonds, J. A., L. E. Clarke, J. P. Lurz, and M. A. Wise. 2007b. "Stabilizing CO_2 Concentrations with Incomplete International Cooperation." Pacific Northwest National Laboratory, Richland, WA. http://www.globalchange.umd.edu/data/publications/PNNL-16932_.pdf.

IPCC (Intergovernmental Panel on Climate Change). 2007. "Climate Change 2007: Synthesis Report. Summary for Policymakers." IPCC, Geneva. http://www.ipcc.ch/pdf/assessment-report/ar4/syr/ar4_syr_spm.pdf.

IWMI (International Water Management Institute). 2007. *Water for Food, Water for Life: A Comprehensive Assessment of Water Management in Agriculture.* London: Earthscan; Colombo: IWMI.

SEG (Scientific Expert Group on Climate Change). 2007. "Confronting Climate Change: Avoiding the Unmanageable and Managing the Unavoidable," ed. Rosina M. Bierbaum, John P. Holdren, Michael C. MacCracken, Richard H. Moss, and Peter H. Raven, prepared for the United Nations Commission on Sustainable Development, Sigma Xi, Research Triangle Park, NC; United Nations Foundation, Washington, DC.

Stern, Nicholas. 2007. *The Economics of Climate Change: The Stern Review.* Cambridge, U.K.: Cambridge University Press.

UNDP (United Nations Development Programme). 2007. *Human Development Report 2007/2008. Fighting Climate Change: Human Solidarity in a Divided World.* New York: UNDP. http://hdr.undp.org/en/media/HDR_20072008_EN_Complete.pdf.

World Bank. 2010. *World Development Report 2010: Development and Climate Change.* Washington, DC: World Bank.

Note

[1] United Nations Framework Convention on Climate Change (UNFCCC), "Greenhouse Gas Inventory Data." http://unfccc.int/ghg_data/items/3800.php.

Keynote Address
Development and Climate Change

JUSTIN YIFU LIN

In order to deal with the implications of climate change for economic development, we must consider all three dimensions of development: economic growth, equity, and sustainability—both social and environmental. Framed in this way, climate change is only one among the many challenges confronting developing countries, which are faced with immediate and pressing needs, limited resources, continued poverty, and social and environmental issues. In many of these countries, human and institutional resources are scarce and overstretched.

That said, climate change could nevertheless be viewed as "the" defining long-term development challenge of the twenty-first century. This position does not imply that the other issues are not big and urgent. Unless, however, we deal with climate change, other development challenges—poverty, inequality, demographic change, public health needs, natural catastrophes, financial and terms-of-trade shocks, and so on—will become even more difficult to manage. Climate change threatens, over time, to reverse the development gains of recent years and limit prospects for further gains. At the same time, we must acknowledge the concern that some policy responses to climate change could be harmful to growth and to poverty alleviation objectives.

After a long buildup of atmospheric carbon dioxide and other greenhouse gases, we now know, in the words of the IPCC (Intergovernmental Panel on Climate Change), that "most of the observed increase in globally averaged temperatures since the mid-20th century is very likely due to the observed increase in anthropogenic greenhouse gas concentrations." We are therefore in a better position than was the case even a few years ago to make it a priority to ask, what are the constraints on resolving climate change challenges? And, given these constraints, what are the most cost-effective, utility-maximizing solutions that we can pursue?

Justin Yifu Lin is chief economist and senior vice president of the World Bank.

Berlin Workshop Series 2010

Although we still have to work hard on filling in the details of these solutions, we know that without effective coordination, it will not be possible to implement the remedies effectively. Limiting atmospheric carbon dioxide and other greenhouse gases to long-term sustainable levels has become one of the most pressing global public goods, and to achieve this aim, coordinated decision making and effective implementation, both globally and at the local level, will be crucial.

I want to begin by discussing what all this means for development institutions, particularly the one I represent—the World Bank—and how we are beginning to respond. I will then briefly review the emerging core messages of the *World Development Report* (*WDR*) and the role that the *WDR* could play in helping define what climate change should mean for the development community. Climate change has been called the greatest market failure of all time. We must make sure that it does not become the greatest governance failure of all time. But without strong, concerted, and well-directed action, we run a great risk of a massive governance failure.

How the World Bank Group Is Addressing the Challenges

All development agencies, and a number of developing-country governments, are struggling today to define how climate change should alter the aid agenda. Climate change is raising many difficult questions. Despite the many and important debates around the economic and technical questions, those aspects are not necessarily where the greatest problems lie. Of more concern is our ability to appropriately respond to the ethical and political questions that climate change raises.

As many have noted, uncertainty is a salient characteristic of climate change. The consequences of these uncertainties have, however, been misunderstood—and, in certain instances, exaggerated. As recognized in the 1992 United Nations Framework Convention on Climate Change, the existence of uncertainties provides motivation for action rather than a case for inaction. As knowledge increases about what kinds of resilience need to be built up, we must at the same time take a hard look at development practice and policy in order to limit maladaptation in the face of continuing uncertainties. This means, for example, rethinking the building of large-scale water supply and irrigation infrastructure where there is significant risk that precipitation will decrease and where underground water resources are already reaching exhaustion, even if the area has been an important center of agricultural activity for a long time.

Climate change is the focus of a huge amount of analysis, capacity building, and development of response options across the world. Within the World Bank Group, as in other international development institutions, multiple efforts are under way—it is rather like seeing a thousand flowers bloom. These efforts all operate under the broad rubric of the World Bank Group's Strategic Framework on Development and Climate Change, which identifies the key development goals of the Bank in responding to climate change and provides a structure for integrating the Bank Group's many initiatives in this area.

Research and analysis includes major bodies of work on the economic and social impacts of climate change, the economics of adaptation to climate change, and policies for disaster risk reduction. Support has been given for studies of prospects for lower-carbon economic growth in several countries (Brazil, India, Indonesia, Mexico, and South Africa), as well as for work on energy policies and other policies for encouraging such growth. These analyses have been carried out at the global, regional, local, and sectoral levels. In addition, the Bank publishes, each year, "State and Trends of the Carbon Market," which reports on the evolution of international "carbon finance" for encouraging mitigation of greenhouse gases in ways that benefit development.

Work on sectoral strategies and policies and on "climate-smart" investments has followed a similar track. Work has been done to strengthen adaptation capacity in, for example, agriculture and water supply, as well as to increase lending and technical assistance for renewable energy and energy efficiency. In 2010 the Bank will rewrite its Energy Strategy, revise its Environment Strategy, and address policies in other key sectors such as water and urban areas. In each instance, the strengthening of components relevant to climate change is a key part of the strategy work. Beyond its own technical and investment programs, the Bank played a central role in developing a Clean Energy Investment Framework (CEIF) to balance environmental sustainability with other key issues such as rural access to energy, especially in Sub-Saharan Africa. And the Bank serves as trustee for the Climate Investment Funds—country-driven efforts to develop innovative measures for climate change mitigation and adaptation.

World Development Report 2010: Goals and Key Messages

The *World Development Report* fits into the World Bank Group's larger approach toward addressing the challenges of climate change. This particular *WDR* has three objectives. The first is to help convince the development community that climate change really does represent a changing environment for development and that "the way we've always done it" is no longer an effective option. The second is to build the case that unless development realities are fully integrated into agreements for mitigating greenhouse gases, those agreements will not deliver significant mitigation or will simply fail. A particular concern in this context is to highlight the importance of ensuring that the voices and interests of poorer and smaller countries are taken into account.

A third goal of the Report is to contribute to the small but growing body of knowledge on how development policy should be designed in a "greenhouse world." In some cases, climate-smart policy will simply entail doing more or better rather than doing something significantly different. In other cases, traditional approaches—for example, managing infrastructure and ecosystems—will need to change more fundamentally. In some instances, difficult trade-offs between more immediate development needs and longer-term climate-related concerns will arise or will be accentuated. These will have to be recognized and addressed through international support, as well as through country-led actions.

Among the many excellent reports on climate change recently published or in preparation, the 2010 *WDR* focuses on what climate change means for development and what development implies for climate change. This is something that few other reports have done—a notable exception being the 2007 *Human Development Report* issued by the United Nations Development Programme (UNDP). In addition, the *WDR* takes an integrated look at adaptation and mitigation, rather than looking at these issues separately. An integrated analysis helps highlight trade-offs, the competition for resources between development and adaptation and mitigation goals, and potential actions with cobenefits. The Report focuses on water, land, and energy as key resources, the supply and demand of which are shifting because of climate change and climate change policies.

The Report presents emerging evidence suggesting that high-income countries have a huge financial stake in reaching an early agreement to limit greenhouse gas emissions in all major economies in order to achieve desired long-term targets for stabilizing the concentration of greenhouse gases in the atmosphere. Delaying incentives for major developing economies to take up low-carbon options could entail enormous deadweight losses for taxpayers in high-income countries as they strive to live within a carbon budget and to lower global emissions. This research suggests that creating financial incentives for major developing countries to join a binding climate agreement with specified targets is not a zero-sum game: major welfare gains are possible. That said, there is a crucial distinction between where emissions are reduced and who finances the reductions, and this divide gets to the heart of both very tough equity issues and the mobilization of international resources for mitigation.

Finally, a central thesis of the Report is that global warming and policies to control it affect the competitive landscape. Climate change will alter the flows of goods and materials worldwide by shifting the most productive agricultural regions and altering water supply and quality. These transformations are likely to affect settlement patterns and migration flows. Climate change will pose new challenges for developing countries but may also create new competitive advantages—for example, in low-carbon energy or in the production of "green" goods that do not sap climate resilience.

While focusing on positive and constructive elements rather than on doom and gloom, this *World Development Report* aims to serve as a call for action. Among the main messages are the following:

1. Climate change is one of many challenges facing developing countries. Unless that reality is well understood and is incorporated into negotiations, those negotiations, which require the active support of developing countries, will fail.

2. Although climate change is only one among many development challenges, it must be tackled soon, or else it will undo development gains and will be difficult to reverse in the future. Growth by itself will not suffice to increase resilience to climate change, for several reasons: growth cannot work fast enough and does not adequately

target the needs of poor people; traditional growth is carbon intensive; and traditional growth strategies can aggravate maladaptation to future change.

3. Climate-smart development is needed and can be achieved. "Climate smart" means more than being climate resilient. It also means seizing opportunities in a changing competitive landscape to strengthen lower-carbon economic growth that benefits developing countries.

4. Although high-income industrial countries must take the lead on mitigation, global greenhouse gas reductions cannot succeed without the active cooperation of middle-income countries. Industrial countries must take the first steps in mitigation because of their much larger annual per capita footprint, their greater capacity to take on the financial and policy burden, and—in the judgment of many—their historical contributions to today's greenhouse gas accumulation. Middle-income countries, however, now account for more than half of the world's annual emissions, and their share is rapidly increasing despite efforts by a number of them to follow lower carbon paths. Mitigation in rich countries alone cannot keep concentrations of greenhouse gases from reaching dangerous levels. The question, then, is not whether developing countries should contribute to the abatement effort, but when and how they can do so while maintaining sufficient space to grow and develop.

The Centrality of Governance

Governance fits into all this because it is the means for implementing solutions to climate challenges. Better governance is important for reducing greenhouse gas emissions effectively and substantially. It is also of fundamental importance in managing climate-induced socioeconomic and ecological impacts. Better governance is required at multiple scales (international to local); in multiple sectors (for example, in energy, agriculture, and other sectors that are characterized by competing demands and differing objectives for mitigation and adaptation); and on the part of multiple actors (both public and private).

"Hard" technological and infrastructure investments are part of the solution to the problems that climate change creates. But technological innovations will require additional incentives, and creating such incentives will not be possible without new policies. Effective infrastructure creation will also require improved governance. Needed changes in behaviors and attitudes will not happen without "soft measures" that strengthen institutions and governance. In short, more effective governance is fundamental in order to avert unmanageable consequences and manage unavoidable impacts of climate change.

This Berlin Conference on Climate Governance and Development is designed to focus on these key themes, with the broad aim of better understanding how climate concerns can be mainstreamed into development. Two principal challenges concern how to manage energy sources and natural resources better. Because the ways in which different sets of actors respond to these challenges will shape the future of a climate-stressed world, the conference includes in-depth consideration of the strengths that various groups of actors can bring to the common goal of creating more effective responses to climate change. This area includes not only policy responses, but also the role of autonomous adaptation to climate change that complements public sector actions or fills in when planned adaptations to climate change fall short.

Effective action will not come about purely through the good will of the different actors involved in creating better ways to address climate challenges. It will also require appropriate financial arrangements at multiple scales. Thus, the conference includes papers on the need for such financial arrangements and on how the appropriate institutional arrangements can be put in place to finance responses to climate change.

Collectively, the papers and the panels assembled for this conference provide a wide-ranging and holistic treatment of different facets of the relationships among climate change, development, and governance. They are certainly a rich feast for those interested in understanding how we can prevent climate change from becoming a governance failure of unprecedented scope and gravity.

Part I
Climate Change as a
Development Priority

Mainstreaming Climate Adaptation into Development: A Policy Dilemma

RICHARD J. T. KLEIN

The need for stronger efforts to support adaptation to climate change in developing countries is undisputed. The potential to create synergies by integrating ("mainstreaming") adaptation into development activities is also widely recognized. Yet, in discussions on the financing of climate adaptation, calls for mainstreaming are viewed with suspicion. Developed countries have committed themselves to providing new and additional finance for adaptation in developing countries, but mainstreaming adaptation into development would make it more difficult to identify whether support for adaptation is indeed new and additional or is, instead, a diversion of existing development finance. This paper outlines that dilemma and calls on developed countries, in particular, the European Union and its member states, to give priority to restoring mutual trust between developed and developing countries in the climate negotiations.

It is now beyond reasonable doubt that climate change is happening, that its cause is the rising concentration of greenhouse gases in the atmosphere, and that these greenhouse gases stem primarily from human activity. The Fourth Assessment Report of the Intergovernmental Panel on Climate Change (IPCC) contained observations of the first effects of climate change. The report concluded that even the most stringent mitigation efforts would not prevent further impacts of climate change in the next few decades (IPCC 2007). This makes adaptation essential, particularly in addressing

Richard J. T. Klein is a senior research fellow at the Stockholm Environment Institute and an adjunct professor at the Centre for Climate Science and Policy Research, Linköping University, Sweden. This paper is an updated version of a briefing note prepared for the European Parliament Temporary Committee on Climate Change. Parts are based on "Adaptation: Needs, Financing and Institutions," prepared for former U.K. Prime Minister Tony Blair by Richard J. T. Klein, Sivan Kartha, Åsa Persson, Paul Watkiss, Frank Ackerman, Thomas E. Downing, Bo Kjellén, and Lisa Schipper. The paper benefited from valuable input from Annett Möhner. Financial support from the European Commission and the Climate Group is gratefully acknowledged, but the views expressed in this chapter are those of the author and do not necessarily reflect the views of these organizations.

Berlin Workshop Series 2010

BOX 1. Mitigation and Adaptation

Action on climate change can take the form of mitigation or adaptation. Mitigation refers to all policies and measures aimed at reducing emissions of greenhouse gases, such as carbon dioxide, or at capturing them in forests, oceans, or underground reservoirs. Adaptation is the term used to describe all activities aimed at preparing for or dealing with the consequences of climate change, be it at the level of individual households, communities, and firms or of entire sectors and countries.

---

near-term impacts. Yet mitigation also remains crucial: to rely on adaptation alone would lead to a level of climate change to which it is no longer possible to effectively adapt, or only at very high social, economic, and environmental costs. Successful action on climate change, therefore, must include both mitigation and adaptation (see box 1).

The effects of climate change will be felt by many groups of society and across many economic sectors. The impacts will include increased water stress, flood risk, food insecurity, reduced biodiversity, loss of livelihoods, economic production losses, increased health risks, and other factors discussed in the IPCC's Fourth Assessment Report. Estimates of the net cost of climate change impacts depend on the rate and magnitude of climate change and on the economic assumptions adopted by the analysts. The assessment report concludes that

- For global average temperature increases of 1–3°C above 1990 levels, both costs and benefits can be expected in different places and sectors.
- For global average temperature increases greater than 2–3°C, it is very likely that all regions will experience either declines in net benefits or increases in net costs.
- Low-latitude and polar regions are projected to experience net costs even for small increases in temperature.

Global mean damage costs could be 1–5 percent of global gross domestic product (GDP) for 4°C of warming, with developing countries expected to experience larger losses. The bigger losses in developing countries come about not only because of their physical characteristics (arid or semiarid land, low-lying coastal areas and flood plains, small islands, and so on), but also because of their greater social and economic vulnerability. In locations with higher exposure and higher sensitivity to climate change impacts, and with low adaptive capacity, the net costs will be significantly larger than the global aggregate. These numbers show that climate change is not only, or even primarily, an environmental challenge: for most of the world it is, above all, a development challenge.

The links between greenhouse gas emissions, mitigation of climate change, and development have been well studied over the years. More recently, the links between adaptation and development have been highlighted. A crucial eye-opener was the report *Poverty and Climate Change: Reducing the Vulnerability of the Poor through Adaptation* (Sperling 2003), prepared by 10 bilateral and multilateral donor organizations in 2003. The report concluded that climate change presents a challenge to the fulfillment of important development objectives, including the United Nations Millennium Development Goals (MDGs), and that pro-poor development is crucial to effective adaptation. Connections between development, adaptation, and basic goals can be fostered through (Sperling 2003)

- *Supporting sustainable livelihoods.* Targeted development efforts help communities enhance social and human capital, preserve and restore natural capital, and secure appropriate physical and financial capital.
- *Ensuring equitable growth.* Growth needs to be fostered in areas of the economy that provide increased employment and higher returns on poor people's assets.
- *Improving governance.* Making public institutions responsive, participative, and accountable to those they serve creates more robust and effective decision-making processes and implementation.

The report concludes that adaptation should be designed to be compatible with development priorities. It presents a strong case for taking climate change into account in development activities, in particular where doing so could add a long-term sustainability component to official development assistance (ODA).

Klein (2001) identifies three areas in which adaptation to climate change is relevant to ODA:

- The risk of climate change to the ODA activity and its deliverables (such as water supply and food security)
- The vulnerability to climate change of the community or ecosystem that is meant to benefit from the ODA activity
- The possible effects of the ODA activity and its deliverables on the vulnerability of communities or ecosystems to climate change.

This paper presents the case for "mainstreaming"—integrating adaptation to climate change into mainstream development planning and decision making. In so doing, it focuses on integration of adaptation into ODA and discusses the process from both an operational and a climate policy perspective. The paper raises two key policy questions associated with mainstreaming and proposes how the European Union (EU) and its member states could address them. First, however, a short summary of the evolution of recent thinking on adaptation to climate change in developing countries is provided.

Adaptation to Climate Change: More Than Technology

The traditional view of adaptation tends to assume that a national government is responsible for implementing technological adaptation measures (for example, provision of seeds, dams, early-warning systems, and irrigation schemes), which are selected on the basis of specific knowledge of future climate conditions (see, for example, Carter et al. 1994). This technology-based view of adaptation has been challenged, for three reasons (see, for example, Smithers and Smit 1997; Burton et al. 2002; Adger et al. 2003).

1. Even though climate science has made great advances over the past years, it is still often difficult to project future impacts of climate change in sufficient detail to justify investment in technological adaptation measures, in particular on a local scale. An important uncertainty relates to the effect of a changing climate on the frequency, magnitude, and spatial occurrence of extreme weather events such as floods, cyclones, and droughts. Planning specific measures on the basis of projections of future climate conditions presents a great challenge for developing countries.

2. Technological adaptation measures can be important in reducing vulnerability to climate change, but they do have their limitations. Three issues need to be considered (Klein et al. 2007):

- Technological adaptation measures may be only partially effective if they do not address nonclimate factors that contribute to vulnerability to climate change. For example, the technological improvement of a water supply system to ensure the availability of water during dry spells will be of limited benefit to people who do not have access to this water. The inequitable distribution of water rights or the price of the water may be more important factors than deficient water supply technology in causing vulnerability to drought.
- Technological adaptation measures may be ineffective if they are not suited to local conditions. For example, new crop varieties may indeed be very resistant to drought, but their acceptance in a community also depends on their costs and availability, farmers' access to fertilizer and other inputs, storage constraints, ease of preparation, flavor, and so on.
- Technological adaptation measures may turn out to be maladaptive if they are implemented without recognition of relevant social and environmental processes. For example, new coastal infrastructure could disturb the offshore sediment balance, resulting in erosion in adjacent coastal areas. Irrigation can lead to the salinization of groundwater and the degradation of wetlands and can reduce subsistence farmers' access to groundwater and productive land.

3. The traditional view of adaptation does not take into account the reliance of adaptation on development, and vice versa. People are vulnerable not only to climate change but also to a range of other stresses, depending on factors such as health status, education, and other socioenvironmental circumstances shaped by political and economic processes (Kelly and Adger 2000; O'Brien et al. 2004). Government initiatives and technological measures designed to adapt to specific changes in climate may therefore fail to address the issues considered most urgent by local communities. These issues may include access to water and food, health and sanitation concerns, and education, as well as livelihood security.

The above analysis leads to the conclusion that an adaptation strategy may need to include measures that address the underlying factors of vulnerability to climate change, particularly on a local scale. These underlying factors are typically structural issues characteristic of low development, such as high dependence on natural resources, resource degradation, inability to secure basic needs, and lack of information and capacity (Sperling 2003). If technological measures are required as a means of reducing vulnerability to climate change, they need to be accompanied by nontechnical measures (for example, training and capacity building; institutional support) to ensure that the technologies are accessible, effective, and suited to local conditions.

Mainstreaming Adaptation into Development

The first empirical studies of climate adaptation (reviewed and assessed for the IPCC's Fourth Assessment Report by Adger et al. 2007) have confirmed that the success of adaptation depends strongly on broader development progress. When adaptation is limited to responses specific to climate change, it neglects the fact that vulnerability to climate change does not emerge in isolation. For example, it may be helpful to provide a rural household that grows a particular subsistence crop with a more drought-resistant variety, but a more robust and comprehensive adaptation strategy would seek to improve food security through a set of coordinated measures that include agricultural extension, crop diversification, integrated pest management, and rainwater harvesting. In addition, a poor rural household is more likely to use these options if it has a literate family member, if it has access to investment capital through local financial institutions, if it can draw on relatively intact social networks, and if it can hold policy makers accountable. In other words, it takes more than narrow, climate-focused measures to build adaptive capacity.

A recent study by the World Resources Institute, *Weathering the Storm: Options for Framing Adaptation and Development* (McGray et al. 2007), provides further confirmation. The study reviewed more than 100 initiatives in developing countries labeled as adaptation and found that in practice, there was little difference between these initiatives and what can be considered good development. The difference lies more in the definition of the problem and the setting of priorities than in the implementation of solutions. The study presents adaptation as a continuum, ranging from more narrowly defined activities aimed specifically at dealing with the impacts of climate change to actions designed to build response capacity and address the drivers of vulnerability (see figure 1).

Mainstreaming adaptation into development can mean different things to different people, depending on whether they hold a technology-based or a development-based view of adaptation. In the technology-based view, mainstreaming largely refers to ensuring that projections of climate change are considered in the decision making of relevant government departments and agencies, so that the technologies chosen are suited to the future climate. For example, in an area projected to experience more intense rainfall events, water managers would fit a drainage system with bigger pipes when replacing old ones, and agricultural extension services concerned about the possibility of increased drought would advise farmers to select crop varieties that are better suited to dry conditions. This type of mainstreaming has also been referred to as "climateproofing" or "mainstreaming minimum." It focuses on the two right-hand boxes in figure 1.

FIGURE 1.
Adaptation as a Continuum

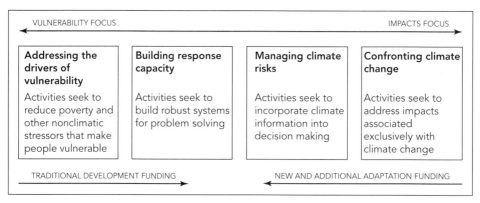

Source: Adapted from McGray, Hammill, and Bradley (2007).

In the development-based view, adaptation to climate change should not be restricted to such things as installing bigger pipes and planting drought-resistant crops but should instead take a comprehensive approach that seeks synergies with development. Mainstreaming can thus ensure that, in addition to climateproofing, development efforts are consciously aimed at reducing vulnerability by incorporating priorities that are critical to successful adaptation, such as ensuring water rights to groups exposed to water scarcity during a drought. This type of mainstreaming, which has been referred to as "mainstreaming plus," focuses on the full continuum of figure 1. It recognizes that adaptation involves many actors, from individual households to national governments, but that an enabling environment needs to be created to ensure that these actors can adapt successfully. This approach includes removing existing financial, legal, institutional, and knowledge barriers to adaptation and strengthening the capacity of people and organizations to adapt.

When linking adaptation with development, it is important to recognize that poverty reduction does not always mean reduction of vulnerability (Adger et al. 2003; Eriksen and Kelly 2007): in that case, synergies between adaptation and development may not exist. There are well-documented instances of activities aimed at reducing poverty that have in fact increased vulnerability. For example, the conversion of mangrove forests into shrimp farms may generate economic gains but leave coastal communities more vulnerable to coastal hazards such as storm surges. New roads in developing countries often affect settlement patterns; even if a new road is constructed so as to withstand climate change, it is equally important to consider whether it would attract new settlers to areas exposed to natural hazards.

If conflicts arise between poverty reduction and vulnerability reduction, adaptation would involve designing and implementing measures that are more targeted to specific threats than development activities tend to be. Mainstreaming can then ensure that development activities themselves are not maladapted to climate change.

Mainstreaming Adaptation from an Operational Perspective

Regardless of whether one holds a technology-based or a development-based view of mainstreaming, it makes common sense from an operational perspective. It is a "no-regrets" approach to making development investments more climateproof and ensuring that they enhance adaptive capacity. The potential for this outcome is considerable.

Many developing countries have already begun to integrate climate risks into their sectoral and national development planning. India, for example, has adopted policies to reduce risks and enhance the adaptive capacity of its most vulnerable sectors and groups. The policies are primarily driven by the objective of ensuring sustainable livelihoods and alleviating poverty. For example, adaptation in the agricultural sector includes the development of drought-resistant crop varieties, the promotion of crop diversification, and the extension of the National Agricultural Insurance Scheme. Overall, India reports spending 2 percent of its GDP on adaptation activities in the areas of agriculture, water resources, health and sanitation, coastal zones, forests, and reduction of disaster risk (Ray 2007).

Since 2001, the least developed countries (LDCs) have been preparing national adaptation programs of action (NAPAs), enabling them to identify priority activities that respond to their urgent and immediate adaptation needs. The rationale for preparing NAPAs is based on the limited ability of LDCs to adapt and the recognition that activities proposed through NAPAs will be those whose further delay could increase vulnerability or lead to increased costs at a later stage. As of February 2010, 44 LDCs had completed their NAPAs, and 36 of these countries are now at various stages of implementing priority activities.

One feature of NAPAs is that they do not establish a parallel planning process but rather attempt to build on national development goals and integrate adaptation into existing national plans. For example, the Gambia established a project steering committee chaired by a permanent secretary, with representatives from the National Assembly and from government departments responsible for budgetary issues, poverty alleviation, and oversight of local government and decentralization. In many LDCs, the NAPA process has strengthened institutional capacity at the national level, thus improving countries' ability to integrate adaptation into sectoral planning and decision making. Rwanda, for example, identifies adaptation as a development priority in its latest economic development and poverty reduction strategy (EDPRS), which covers the period 2008–11. The aim is to develop sectoral strategies to implement the EDRPS while taking into account the priorities identified in Rwanda's NAPA.

In spite of these efforts by developing countries, in many cases, external support will be required to meet adaptation needs. ODA is already an important source of income for many LDCs, and it can play a major part in supporting adaptation. The Organisation for Economic Co-operation and Development (OECD) estimates that in Nepal, for example, as much as 50–65 percent of total ODA is directed to activities potentially affected by climate risks (Agrawala 2005). There is potential for more than 60 percent of all ODA from OECD countries to contribute positively toward

---

BOX 2. Mainstreaming in Official Development Assistance

Discussions on mainstreaming are most advanced in the context of official development assistance (ODA), which still contributes a substantial share of the income of many developing countries, particularly those in the least developed group. In April 2006 the Organisation for Economic Co-operation and Development (OECD) held a ministerial-level meeting of its Development Assistance Committee (DAC) and its Environment Policy Committee (EPOC). The meeting, which launched a process of working in partnership with developing countries to integrate environmental factors efficiently into national development policies and poverty reduction strategies, yielded an agreed Framework for Common Action around Shared Goals and a Declaration on Integrating Climate Change Adaptation into Development Cooperation. These outcomes are providing an impetus for all development agencies to consider climate change in their operations and thus facilitate mainstreaming. A recent publication (OECD 2009) provides policy guidance for doing so.

---

adaptation and adaptive capacity. This potential is now being recognized by donor agencies (see box 2).

Several donor agencies have begun screening their portfolios for mainstreaming opportunities. Klein et al. (2007) analyzed the six portfolio screenings that were publicly available by 2006, focusing on both the results and the methods applied. The six screenings were conducted independently and therefore used different methods, but they all pursued the same two goals:

- To ascertain the extent to which existing development activities already consider climate risks or address vulnerability to climate change
- To identify opportunities for incorporating climate change into future activities

Klein et al. (2007) found that climate change was initially almost absent from the agencies' activities. Where it was mentioned, it was framed as an issue of mitigation and was in the domain of environment ministries and departments. Notably, little connection to climate change was made in areas where the climate already poses clear risks today. Since the initial screenings, however, the situation has changed considerably—the result of an increased understanding of the need for mainstreaming and what such mainstreaming would entail for donor agencies. In addition to screening their portfolios, donor agencies have now begun to screen individual projects to find out whether

- Climate change could pose a risk to meeting the objectives and producing the deliverables of the project
- Concrete adaptations and measures to strengthen adaptive capacity could be incorporated into the project design
- The project might increase the exposure of people and economic assets to climate risk and so turn out to be maladaptive

Mainstreaming Adaptation from a Climate Policy Perspective

As was seen above, mainstreaming adaptation into development makes common sense from an operational perspective. It also makes sense from a development policy perspective. After all, the integration of similar policy objectives into one operational program leads to a more efficient use of financial and human resources than if adaptation were designed, implemented, and managed separately from ongoing development planning and decision making. Such integration reduces transaction costs and improves the effectiveness of aid. But from a climate policy perspective, mainstreaming creates a dilemma. Financial flows for adaptation and those for development (for example, ODA) are managed separately, as a result of climate policy negotiations. It is as yet unclear whether and how the separate funds could be combined.

Article 4.4 of the United Nations Framework Convention on Climate Change (UNFCCC) commits developed countries to assist those developing-country parties that are particularly vulnerable to the adverse effects of climate change in meeting costs of adaptation to those adverse effects. This assistance is understood to come in the form of new and additional funding (that is, beyond what developed countries are already planning to provide as ODA).

In 2001 the Conference of the Parties (COP) to the UNFCCC established three funds to support adaptation activities in developing countries: the Least Developed Countries Fund and the Special Climate Change Fund, under the UNFCCC, and the Adaptation Fund, under the Kyoto Protocol. The two funds under the UNFCCC are operational and are managed by the Global Environment Facility (GEF)—as is the Strategic Priority on "Piloting an Operational Approach to Adaptation" (SPA), which the GEF established under its Trust Fund. The operational GEF funds provide funding to eligible countries to meet the additional costs of adaptation. The remaining costs are to be borne by the recipient country, by other bilateral or multilateral donors, or by both. As of October 2009, US$287.4 million had been pledged for adaptation under the Least Developed Countries Fund and the Special Climate Change Fund; of this amount, US$180.8 million has been allocated. The SPA has allocated all US$50 million it had available (GEF 2009; UNFCCC 2009).

The Adaptation Fund became operational in 2009. As was decided by the COP serving as the Meeting of the Parties to the Kyoto Protocol (CMP) in 2007, it is managed by a special Adaptation Fund Board (AFB), which has prepared specific operational policies and guidelines for the fund (AFB 2009). The Adaptation Fund is the first financial instrument under the UNFCCC and its Kyoto Protocol that is not based solely on voluntary contributions from donor countries. It receives a 2 percent share of proceeds from project activities under the Clean Development Mechanism (CDM) and can also receive funds from other sources to fund concrete adaptation projects and programs. The actual amount of money that will be available from the Adaptation Fund depends on the extent to which the CDM is used and on the price of carbon. Estimates vary from US$80 million to US$300 million per year during the period 2008–12 (UNFCCC 2009).

Despite the existence of these dedicated funds, developing countries are concerned that, as a result of donors' seeking to create synergies between adaptation and development investments, funding for adaptation will not be new and additional but, in effect, will be absorbed into ODA budgets of a fixed size. The concern is fueled by the fact that the amount of money available in the new funds is only a fraction of the estimated investment needs in developing countries (see box 3). Moreover, only a few countries have achieved the target, reaffirmed most recently in 2002 at the Conference on Development Financing in Monterrey, Mexico, of providing ODA equal to 0.7 percent of gross national income. A second, related concern is that mainstreaming could divert any new and additional funds for adaptation into more general development activities, thus limiting the opportunity to evaluate, at least quantitatively, their benefits with respect to climate change specifically. Third, there is concern that donors' use of ODA to pursue mainstreamed adaptation could impose conditionalities on what should be a country-driven process.

BOX 3. Investment for Adaptation: Some Cost Estimates

Adaptation to climate change will impose additional costs on both the public and private sectors. In the past few years, a number of organizations have published estimates of these costs. The United Nations Framework Convention on Climate Change (UNFCCC) Secretariat estimates the additional investment and financial flows needed worldwide in 2030 to be US$60 billion–US$182 billion (UNFCCC 2007). The largest uncertainty in this estimate is in the cost of adapting infrastructure; that investment may require anything from US$8 billion to US$130 billion in 2030, one-third of which would be for developing countries. The UNFCCC also estimates that an additional US$52 billion–US$62 billion would be needed for agriculture, water, health, ecosystem protection, and coastal zone protection; most of this would be used in developing countries. In total, US$28 billion to US$67 billion in additional investment and financial flows would be needed for adaptation in developing countries in 2030.

Others arrive at similar estimates. The World Bank (2006) concludes that the incremental costs of adapting to the projected impacts of climate change in developing countries are likely to be in the order of US$9 billion to US$41 billion per year, while Oxfam International (2007) estimates the figure at more than US$50 billion per year. The United Nations Development Programme (UNDP 2007) suggests that by 2015, financing requirements for adaptation in developing countries could amount to US$86 billion–US$109 billion per year. Parry et al. (2009), however, suggest that these estimates are too low. They conclude that the UNFCCC estimate of investment needs is probably an underestimate by a factor of between 2 and 3 for the included sectors; it could be much more if other sectors are considered as well.

The Bali Action Plan and Beyond

With the Bali Action Plan, agreed on in December 2007, the COP launched "a comprehensive process to enable the full, effective and sustained implementation of the Convention through long-term cooperative action, now, up to and beyond 2012, in order to reach an agreed outcome and adopt a decision at its fifteenth session" in Copenhagen in December 2009 (COP15). The Bali Action Plan attaches equal weight to mitigation and adaptation and identifies technology and finance as the key mechanisms for enabling developing countries to respond to climate change. It recognizes the need for action to enhance adaptation in five main areas:

- International cooperation to support urgent implementation of adaptation actions, through vulnerability assessments, prioritization of actions, financial needs assessments, capacity building, and integration of adaptation actions into sectoral and national planning
- Risk management and risk reduction strategies, including risk-sharing and transfer mechanisms such as insurance
- Disaster reduction strategies and means for addressing loss and damage associated with climate change impacts in developing countries that are particularly vulnerable to climate change
- Economic diversification to build resilience
- Strengthening of the catalytic role of the UNFCCC in encouraging multilateral bodies, the public and private sectors, and civil society to build on synergies among activities and processes in order to support adaptation in a coherent and integrated manner.

In the event, no agreed outcome was reached at COP15, and no comprehensive decision was adopted that included these five issues. Instead, the COP decided to take note of the Copenhagen Accord, a nonbinding political declaration about which there was no consensus among parties. Yet work is already under way on the five issues, both under the auspices of the UNFCCC and independently from it. This work needs to continue, but greater efforts are needed to clarify the links between adaptation finance and development assistance. With respect to mainstreaming, in particular, it is necessary to address two questions (Persson and Klein 2009; Persson et al. 2009):

- Should adaptation be designed as stand-alone activities, or should it be mainstreamed into development projects and programs?
- Should the provision of support for adaptation follow the polluter-pays principle, or is adaptation an additional focus of ODA?

In reality these are not either-or questions; the answers depend on the type of adaptation being considered and on the purpose adaptation is trying to serve (see figure 1). However, pre-Copenhagen negotiations under the UNFCCC, and, in particular, those on adaptation funding for developing countries, left little room for such nuance. As mentioned above, developing countries are concerned that efforts to promote the mainstreaming of adaptation are a ploy by developed countries to avoid providing new and additional funding for adaptation. As recently as the UNFCCC subsidiary bodies' meeting in June 2008, developing countries called for stand-alone adaptation activities because these would allow for the measurable, reportable, and verifiable use of new and additional funding, as stipulated in the Bali Action Plan.

Thus, the first question is linked to the second, which shows that the operational perspective of mainstreaming ("common sense") cannot be separated from the climate policy perspective ("new and additional funding"). Both the current setup of adaptation funding under the UNFCCC and the fact that ODA is gradually being used less to support project-based activities and more to provide program and budget support make mainstreaming difficult in practice. At the same time, the need for adaptation investments in developing countries is becoming increasingly evident, and the willingness of developed countries to make funds available is increasing. One bottleneck is the problem of reaching agreement on how to fund adaptation under the UNFCCC. Table 1 summarizes the pros and cons of stand-alone adaptation and mainstreamed adaptation in the context of adaptation funding.

Regardless of whether they are used to support stand-alone or mainstreamed activities, existing resources fall short of the estimated costs of adaptation by roughly two orders of magnitude (see box 3). The Copenhagen Accord recognizes that substantially greater financial resources are needed and includes the goal of mobilizing US$100 billion a year by 2020 to address the needs of developing countries. To this end it establishes the Copenhagen Green Climate Fund. In addition, it mentions the provision of new and additional resources approaching US$30 billion for the period 2010–12, with balanced allocation between adaptation and mitigation. The nonbinding status of the Copenhagen Accord, the uncertain origin of the money, and the history of pledges not honored, however, have led to skepticism that these amounts will be made available and, if so, that they will be new and additional resources.

A number of developed countries and development banks are setting up separate ODA-based funds that could also support adaptation activities in developing countries, thus complementing (or competing with) the GEF funds and the Adaptation Fund. Large initiatives include the Pilot Program for Climate Resilience administered

TABLE 1. Stand-Alone Adaptation and Mainstreamed Adaptation Compared

	Stand-alone adaptation	Mainstreamed adaptation
Pros	Easy to calculate new and additional funding needs Greater country ownership	More efficient in implementation More effective, more sustainable impact
Cons	High administrative costs when scaled up Potential conflict with development objectives	Difficult funding situation, possibly diverting ODA Seen as imposing conditionalities

Source: Author's elaboration.

Note: ODA, official development assistance.

by the World Bank, with a total budget of US$614 million for eight selected countries and two small-island regions; the United Nations Development Programme (UNDP)–Spain MDG Achievement Fund, with up to US$90 million over four years; the German International Climate Initiative (up to US$240 million over four years); and the European Commission's Global Climate Change Alliance (GCCA) (up to US$140 million over three years). An up-to-date overview of all climate funds is maintained by the U.K. Overseas Development Institute.[1]

Developing countries and some observers have expressed concern that these new funds are donor driven, that money will in part be made available as loans instead of grants, and that possible competition between these funds and those under the UNFCCC and the Kyoto Protocol may lead to a decoupling of adaptation and mitigation in the climate negotiations (South Centre 2009). Such decoupling could undermine the developing countries' position that support for adaptation is a moral and legal imperative for the developed countries and has to go hand in hand with emission reductions. The outcome might be a weakening of the carbon market—the most likely source of adaptation finance not counted as ODA. In theory, the carbon market could make a future climate agreement self-financing: that is, if emission targets were ambitious, the price of carbon would rise significantly, which would increase financial flows to developing countries.

The Adaptation Fund is the first example of the use of market-based options to generate substantial financial resources to address climate change (as opposed to using ODA). However, instead of taxing carbon emissions (which would be in line with the polluter-pays principle), it taxes carbon exchanges, creating a disincentive to investments in developing countries. Nonetheless, developing countries and many nongovernmental organizations see the institutional setup of the Adaptation Fund as superior to the arrangements for the separate funds that are being established. In particular, the direct representation of developing countries on the Adaptation Fund Board and the fact that applicant countries can choose their own implementing entities are seen as strong improvements on the existing GEF-managed funds under the UNFCCC. The GEF has been criticized for the way it has managed those funds (see, for example, Möhner and Klein 2007; South Centre 2008; Klein and Möhner 2009), and if rumors in the corridors are anything to go by, the GEF has yet to gain widespread support for its role as the secretariat of the Adaptation Fund Board.

Müller (2008) presents and evaluates various options for generating substantially more funding for adaptation, in addition to the 2 percent levy on the CDM. These options vary from imposing levies on airline tickets and earmarking part of the proceeds of the auctioning of emission rights, to setting a percentage target of developed countries' GDP, similar to the current ODA target. Regardless of the preferred ways of generating funds, adaptation financing needs to evolve into an arrangement in which parties accept binding commitments to contribute resources toward adaptation. At the Bali meeting, the parties to the UNFCCC (2009) reiterated the need for such steps, calling for "adequate, predictable, and sustainable financial resources." To rely on ad hoc, discretionary contributions is to risk a perennial shortfall in resources.

A principle-based and transparent process for determining national burden-sharing contributions to international adaptation funding is necessary, and there is a legal basis for this. A universal ethical principle holds that it is wrong to harm others (or to risk harming them) for one's own gain and that one owes compensation if one does such harm. Over time, this moral principle has become firmly encoded in national case law and legal reasoning with respect to environmental pollution within national boundaries. International law echoes the same principle. In the Stockholm Declaration of 1972, principle 21 (reaffirmed in principle 2 of the Rio Declaration in 1992) affirms that states have "the responsibility to ensure that activities within their jurisdiction or control do not cause damage to the environment of other States or of areas beyond the limits of national jurisdiction." Principle 22 of the Stockholm Declaration provides that "States shall cooperate to develop further the international law regarding liability and compensation for the victims of pollution and other environmental damage caused by activities within the jurisdiction or control of such States to areas beyond their jurisdiction."

European Policy and Practice: Current Efforts and Future Directions

Mainstreaming can be beneficial to developed and developing countries alike. For example, the European Commission has made progress on adaptation through the European Climate Change Programme's Working Group on Impacts and Adaptation. This group is mandated "to integrate adaptation fully into relevant European policy areas, to identify good, cost-effective practice in the development of adaptation policy, and to foster learning." The working group provided input to the European Commission's preparation in 2007 of a Green Paper on adaptation, which was followed by a White Paper in 2009. The White Paper (European Commission 2009a) sets out a framework for reducing the EU's vulnerability to the impact of climate change and emphasizes the possibilities for integrating adaptation into sectoral planning and decision making.

The main focus of the White Paper is on adaptation within the EU and its member states, but it also contains a section on the external dimension and on ongoing work under the UNFCCC. The paper states that "external EU policy should also make a substantial contribution to adaptation, via water management, agriculture, biodiversity, forests, desertification, energy, health, social policy, research, coastal erosion, and disaster risk reduction." It cites the GCCA as a means of supporting adaptation in developing countries, in particular LDCs and small island developing states (SIDS).

Another relevant communication by the European Commission, "Towards a Comprehensive Climate Change Agreement in Copenhagen" (European Commission 2009b), addresses explicitly the EU position in the climate negotiations under the UNFCCC. It reaffirms that financial and technological support should be provided to the most vulnerable countries, in particular LDCs and SIDS. It also states that there should be a transition from project-based approaches to adaptation toward long-term strategic integration in a country's broader planning and development strategy. However, other than a reference to the potential usefulness of experience gained through the GCCA, no concrete steps are proposed.

A much larger effort is required of the EU and its member states in supporting adaptation and mainstreaming in developing countries. First, the EU and its member states will need to clarify their position concerning the two questions posed in the previous section. As for the first question ("Should adaptation be designed as stand-alone activities, or should it be mainstreamed into development projects and programs?"), there is no need to make an a priori decision for one or the other. Rather, the choice should be an outcome of a country-driven national planning process. National adaptation planning in developing countries needs to be supported under the UNFCCC, and developed countries must provide follow-up support to implement adaptation activities identified in these national plans. The GCCA could become an important European instrument for providing such follow-up, provided that its budget is substantially increased. As for the second question ("Should the provision of support for adaptation follow the polluter-pays principle, or is adaptation an additional focus of ODA?"), whether ODA or new and additional funding is most appropriate for supporting adaptation to climate change depends on the nature of the adaptation activities. ODA could be used to support activities that fit in the two boxes on the left-hand side of figure 1 (addressing the drivers of vulnerability and building response capacity), and new and additional funding could support activities corresponding to the two boxes on the right-hand side (managing climate risks and confronting climate change). The EU and its member states should clarify how traditional ODA, the Adaptation Fund, the Copenhagen Green Climate Fund, and various other bilateral and multilateral funds for adaptation can complement one another. In addition, they should address concerns that mainstreaming adaptation might not lead to new and additional funding. The GCCA could play a role in providing such clarity and addressing the concerns.

In addition, the EU and its member states (and, indeed, all developed countries) should accept a transparent, principle-based allocation of responsibility for adaptation funding, resulting in adequate, new, and additional money to support adaptation programs in developing countries. Levies on carbon market transactions and auctions of emission permits are two existing mechanisms for generating new and additional funds, the latter of which is consistent with the polluter-pays principle. The use of such mechanisms needs to be expanded. In addition, the EU's overall ODA should reach 0.7 percent of gross EU income, without including new and additional funds generated by the carbon market. In collaboration with the OECD Development Assistance Committee, the EU should develop guidance for bilateral donor agencies to ensure that funding for adaptation is reported consistently in all member states.

Finally, the EU and its member states need to invest in building trust with the developing countries. Regardless of the direction of the current discussions, any post-Copenhagen agreement is clouded by a lack of trust between developed and developing countries. Questions of equity and fairness in climate policy extend to virtually all agreements that require North–South cooperation. Within climate policy, developing countries question the good faith of developed countries because of the failure of many of them to meet their Kyoto commitments. As mentioned above, there is also little faith in the promise of new and additional finance for developing countries. Despite the strong global consensus behind the MDGs, the financial resources required to meet these goals have not materialized (and neither have the necessary institutional and governance changes). Earlier, the achievement of the Agenda 21 targets adopted at the Rio Earth Summit in 1992 was hindered by a lack of financial resources, and only a few countries have met the target reaffirmed most recently in Monterrey of providing 0.7 percent of gross national income as conventional ODA.

Another potential area of distrust on the side of developing countries is the neutrality of processes or institutions through which agreements are implemented, money is disbursed, and disagreements are resolved. Questions concern not only the neutrality of international financial institutions but also donor conditionalities. The lack of trust will hobble any future agreement on climate finance unless developed countries can gain trust by addressing developing countries' concerns regarding equity, fairness, and the neutrality of institutions.

Note

1. The overview is available at http://www.climatefundsupdate.org/.

References

Adger, W. Neil, Saleemul Huq, Katrina Brown, Declan Conway, and Mike Hulme. 2003. "Adaptation to Climate Change in the Developing World." *Progress in Development Studies* 3 (3): 179–95.

Adger, W. Neil, Shardul Agrawala, Monirul M. Q. Mirza, Cecilia Conde, Karen O'Brien, Juan Pulhin, Roger Pulwarty, Barry Smit, and Kiyoshi Takahashi. 2007. "Assessment of Adaptation Practices, Options, Constraints, and Capacity." In *Climate Change 2007: Impacts, Adaptation and Vulnerability. Contribution of Working Group II to the Fourth Assessment Report of the Intergovernmental Panel on Climate Change*, ed. Martin L. Parry, Osvaldo F. Canziani, Jean P. Palutikof, Paul J. van der Linden, and Claire E. Hanson, 717–43. Cambridge, U.K.: Cambridge University Press.

AFB (Adaptation Fund Board). 2009. *Accessing Resources from the Adaptation Fund: The Handbook*. Washington, DC: Adaptation Fund Board Secretariat.

Agrawala, Shardul, ed. 2005. *Bridge over Troubled Waters: Linking Climate Change and Development*. Paris: Organisation for Economic Co-operation and Development (OECD) Publishing.

Burton, Ian, Saleemul Huq, Bo Lim, Olga Pilifosova, and Emma Lisa Schipper. 2002. "From Impacts Assessment to Adaptation Priorities: The Shaping of Adaptation Policy." *Climate Policy* 2 (2–3): 145–59.

Carter, Tim L., Martin L. Parry, Shuzo Nishioka, and Hideo Harasawa, eds. 1994. *IPCC Technical Guidelines for Assessing Climate Change Impacts and Adaptations*. Report of Working Group II of the Intergovernmental Panel on Climate Change. London: University College London; Tsukuba, Japan: Centre for Global Environmental Research.

Eriksen, Siri E. H., and P. Mick Kelly. 2007. "Developing Credible Vulnerability Indicators for Policy Assessment." *Mitigation and Adaptation Strategies for Global Change* 12 (4): 495–524.

European Commission. 2009a. "Adapting to Climate Change: Towards a European Framework for Action." White Paper, COM (2009) 147/4, European Commission, Brussels.

———. 2009b. "Towards a Comprehensive Climate Change Agreement in Copenhagen." COM (2009) 39, European Commission, Brussels. http://ec.europa.eu/environment/climat/pdf/future_action/communication.pdf.

GEF (Global Environment Facility). 2009. "Status Report on the Special Climate Change Fund and the Least Developed Countries Fund." GEF/LDCF.SCCF.7/Inf.2, GEF Secretariat, Washington, DC.

IPCC (Intergovernmental Panel on Climate Change). 2007. "Summary for Policymakers." In *Climate Change 2007: Impacts, Adaptation and Vulnerability. Contribution of Working Group II to the Fourth Assessment Report of the Intergovernmental Panel on Climate Change*, ed. Martin L. Parry, Osvaldo F. Canziani, Jean P. Palutikof, Paul J. van der Linden, and Claire E. Hanson, 7–22. Cambridge, U.K.: Cambridge University Press.

Kelly, P. Mick, and W. Neil Adger. 2000. "Theory and Practice in Assessing Vulnerability to Climate Change and Facilitating Adaptation." *Climatic Change* 47 (4): 325–52.

Klein, Richard J. T. 2001. "Adaptation to Climate Change in German Official Development Assistance—An Inventory of Activities and Opportunities, with a Special Focus on Africa." Deutsche Gesellschaft für Technische Zusammenarbeit, Eschborn, Germany.

Klein, Richard J. T., and Annett Möhner. 2009. "Governance Limits to Effective Global Financial Support for Adaptation." In *Adapting to Climate Change: Thresholds, Values, Governance*, ed. W. Neil Adger, Irene Lorenzoni, and Karen L. O'Brien, 465–75. Cambridge, U.K.: Cambridge University Press.

Klein, Richard J. T., Siri E. H. Eriksen, Lars Otto Næss, Anne Hammill, Thomas M. Tanner, Carmenza Robledo, and Karen L. O'Brien. 2007. "Portfolio Screening to Support the Mainstreaming of Adaptation to Climate Change into Development Assistance." *Climatic Change* 84 (1): 23–44.

McGray, Heather, Anne Hammill, Rob Bradley, E. Lisa, F. Schipper, and Jo-Ellen Parry. 2007. *Weathering the Storm: Options for Framing Adaptation and Development*. Washington, DC: World Resources Institute.

Möhner, Annett, and Richard J. T. Klein. 2007. "The Global Environment Facility: Funding for Adaptation or Adapting to Funds?" Climate and Energy Programme Working Paper, Stockholm Environment Institute, Stockholm.

Müller, Benito. 2008. "International Adaptation Finance: The Need for an Innovative and Strategic Approach." Working Paper EV 42, Oxford Institute for Energy Studies, Oxford, U.K.

O'Brien, Karen, Siri Eriksen, Ane Schjolden, and Lynn P. Nygaard. 2004. "What's in a Word? Conflicting Interpretations of Vulnerability in Climate Change Research." CICERO Working Paper 2004: 4, Centre for International Climate and Environmental Research Oslo (CICERO), University of Oslo.

OECD (Organisation for Economic Co-operation and Development). 2009. "Policy Guidance on Integrating Climate Change Adaptation into Development Co-operation." Development Assistance Committee and Environmental Policy Committee, OECD, Paris.

Oxfam International. 2007. "Adapting to Climate Change: What's Needed in Poor Countries, and Who Should Pay." Oxfam Briefing Paper 104, Oxfam International Secretariat, Oxford, U.K.

Parry, Martin, Nigel Arnell, Pam Berry, David Dodman, Samuel Fankhauser, Chris Hope, Sari Kovats, Robert Nicholls, David Satterthwaite, Richard Tiffin, and Tim Wheeler. 2009.

Assessing the Costs of Adaptation to Climate Change: A Review of the UNFCCC and Other Recent Estimates. London: International Institute for Environment and Development.

Persson, Åsa, and Richard J. T. Klein. 2009. "Mainstreaming Adaptation to Climate Change into Official Development Assistance: Challenges to Foreign Policy Integration." In *Climate Change and Foreign Policy: Case Studies from East to West*, ed. P. Harris, London: Routledge.

Persson, Åsa, Richard J. T. Klein, Clarisse Kehler Siebert, Aaron Atteridge, Benito Müller, Juan Hoffmaister, Michael Lazarus, and Takeshi Takama. 2009. *Adaptation Finance under a Copenhagen Agreed Outcome.* Stockholm: Stockholm Environment Institute.

Ray, Rajasree. 2007. "India: Adaptation Approaches and Strategies." Presentation at the Third Workshop, United Nations Framework Convention on Climate Change (UNFCCC) Dialogue on Long-Term Cooperative Action to Address Climate Change by Enhancing Implementation of the Convention, Bonn, Germany, May 17.

Smithers, John, and Barry Smit. 1997. "Human Adaptation to Climatic Variability and Change." *Global Environmental Change* 7 (2): 129–46.

South Centre. 2008: "The Administrative Costs of Climate Change Adaptation Financing: The Global Environment Facility as an Operating Entity of the UNFCCC Financial Mechanism." Analytical Note SC/GDDP/AN/ENV/4. South Centre. Geneva.

———. 2009. "Developed Country Climate Financing Initiatives Weaken the UNFCCC." Analytical Note SC/GGDP/AN/ENV/7. South Centre. Geneva.

Sperling, Frank, ed. 2003. *Poverty and Climate Change: Reducing the Vulnerability of the Poor through Adaptation.* African Development Bank, Asian Development Bank, UK Department for International Development, Directorate General for Development (European Commission), Bundesministerium für wirtschaftliche Zusammenarbeit und Entwicklung (Germany), Directorate-General of Development Cooperation (the Netherlands), OECD, UNDP, United Nations Environment Programme, and World Bank, Washington, DC.

UNDP (United Nations Development Programme). 2007. *Human Development Report 2007/2008. Fighting Climate Change: Human Solidarity in a Divided World.* Basingstoke, U.K.: Palgrave Macmillan.

UNFCCC (United Nations Framework Convention on Climate Change). 2007. "Investment and Financial Flows to Address Climate Change." UNFCCC Secretariat, Bonn, Germany.

———. 2009. "Investment and Financial Flows to Address Climate Change: An Update." UNFCCC Secretariat, Bonn, Germany.

World Bank. 2006. "Clean Energy and Development: Towards an Investment Framework." World Bank, Washington, DC.

Part II
Energy and Development:
Policies and Technologies

Urbanization and Sustainable Cities: The Role of Governance, Infrastructure, and Technology

JUDITH A. LAYZER

Cities will be critical to the quest for sustainability in the twenty-first century. Over-exploiting nonrenewable resources and using remote places as sources of raw materials and as waste sinks are no longer options, for both economic and ecological reasons. The developing world will need an entirely new model of urban development, based not on fossil fuels and export-driven economic growth but on integrated systems of local power generation, food production, water management, and waste reuse and recycling. Because cities concentrate populations in small areas, they have the potential to achieve energy efficiencies and preserve the surrounding countryside.

Tough challenges stand in the way to this kind of future. The global economy is currently built on ever-increasing, pollution-generating consumption. Many object, too, that developing countries have more pressing priorities than sustainability. Local leadership that puts sustainability at the top of its agenda, bolstered by international funding for locally appropriate infrastructure and technology, will be an essential feature of governance in the world's emerging sustainable cities.

Cities will be critical to the quest for sustainability in the twenty-first century. More than half of the world's people live in urban areas. In developed countries, the figure is closer to three-quarters, and demographers predict that almost all the population growth over the next 40 years is likely to occur in developing-country cities. Today's large cities became wealthy by overexploiting nonrenewable resources and by using remote places as sources of raw materials and as waste sinks—a path that is no longer an option, for both economic and ecological reasons. The developing world will need an entirely new model of urban development, a trajectory, based not on fossil fuels and export-driven economic growth but on integrated systems of local

Judith A. Layzer is an associate professor of environmental policy in the Department of Urban Studies and Planning, Massachusetts Institute of Technology, Cambridge, MA.

Berlin Workshop Series 2010

power generation, food production, water management, and waste reuse and recycling. Local leadership that puts sustainability at the top of its agenda, bolstered by international funding for locally appropriate infrastructure and technology, will be an essential feature of governance in the world's emerging sustainable cities.

Urbanization and Sustainability

For some, "urban sustainability" is an oxymoron because, historically, cities have been sources of environmental problems. Cities disrupt biogeochemical cycles—for example, by compacting soils and creating microclimates such as heat islands and air-pollution hot spots. In addition, cities remove nutrients from the landscape and concentrate them as waste, which they then treat and dump in landfills or send to the sea, depleting agricultural soils in the process. In an effort to revitalize those soils, farmers use chemical fertilizers whose production and disposition impose huge costs on agricultural workers and the environment. In the United States, for example, the 6,000-square-mile Chesapeake Bay ecosystem is collapsing, in large part because of nutrients running off farm fields and into rivers that feed the bay.

Cities also disrupt aquatic cycles by disturbing water flows above and below ground. Typically, cities begin by exploiting their local groundwater supplies. Once local aquifers become depleted or contaminated, cities lay claim to water from distant sources. Meanwhile, urban developers create impervious surfaces, which dramatically reduce the natural seepage that would purify that water and replenish local aquifers. The changes in the water table that result from these actions threaten urban infrastructure, the reliability of the clean water supply, and the resilience of cities in the face of an increasingly volatile climate.

In addition to their effects on the local environment, contemporary cities are consumption hubs that rely heavily on global trade for their prosperity. Urban dwellers, particularly in the developing world, consume more resources than their rural counterparts, and urban metabolism studies—which measure the throughput of resources such as water, energy, and materials—show that per capita consumption in cities has been increasing steadily since the 1970s.

At a more subtle level, cities have the psychological effect of removing their inhabitants from the natural systems they rely on. As a result, city dwellers are much less aware than rural ones of their dependence on functioning natural systems, making it more difficult to change behavior.

Paradoxically, though, cities are an essential part of the global effort to become more sustainable. Urban form strongly affects residents' demands for natural resources, particularly energy, but also water and land, as well as wood and other raw materials. Cities that are dense and are served by well-designed transit systems use far less energy than suburban or rural developments. In this regard, Manhattan in New York City is an ecotopia: 82 percent of Manhattanites get to work by public transit, by bicycle, or on foot. Many live in apartments, thereby minimizing their individual heating and cooling requirements. Compact cities also reduce consumption of land on the periphery—land that provides valuable ecological services such as air and water filtration, as well as habitat for nonhuman species and respite for people. Importantly, undeveloped land absorbs carbon dioxide, reducing the impact of urban emissions.

Because of their relative density, cities require less infrastructure per square mile to move water and waste around. They can install large-scale systems for conserving and reusing water, transporting sewage, and recycling and reusing materials. They also furnish opportunities for cogeneration, which turns process-waste heat from industry and power generation into energy. Cities even help curb population growth, as urban dwellers tend to have fewer children.

In short, cities have the potential for great ecoefficiencies. But the growth of twentieth-century cities, and their ability to resolve the immediate health threats posed by wastes and lack of clean water, rested on fossil fuel consumption and a parasitic reliance on the resources of remote locations for material inputs and waste disposal. Such an approach is no longer possible, both because there are no more "elsewheres" and because—thanks to population pressures and economic growth— resource shortages and the resulting high resource prices will preclude it.

The metaphor of leapfrogging stages of industrial development is probably not helpful. Instead, a sustainable development model for the twenty-first century should entail an entirely different trajectory, one that explicitly integrates the "green" agenda of developed nations (managing the human impact on the environment) with the "brown" agenda of developing countries, focusing on sanitation, health, and access to clean water. In such a model, developing countries would meet the needs of the poorest citizens, while avoiding the wasteful choices whose consequences developed countries are currently trying to overcome. In fact, the problems posed by contemporary cities provide a starting point. Rather than removing nutrients from distant ecosystems, developing cities could pioneer systems for producing food regionally; rather than concentrating and disposing of waste, they could establish processes for reusing, composting, and recycling biological and technical materials; and, rather than creating energy- and chemical-intensive water and sanitation systems, they could invest in simpler, more biologically based systems.

Governance, Infrastructure, and Technology

What, then, will be the features of the sustainable twenty-first-century city? Such a city will be powered primarily by the sun and wind but will also draw on geothermal heating and cooling and, in coastal areas, the tides. Cogeneration will be the norm, not a boutique exception. Technology to address residents' basic needs will consist of creative and locally appropriate solutions—not always the most complex or expensive ones—as the engineering emphasis shifts from control of nature to biomimicry and working with nature. Curitiba, Brazil, provides an instructive example: rather than invest huge sums in a high-technology transportation system, Curitiba created a bus–rapid-transit system that has become a global model. Similarly, in thinking about devising new technologies (and disseminating existing ones), we should beware the fixation on "scaling up"; in many cases what cities should aim for is a mix of small-scale and medium-scale solutions, tailored to particular circumstances, rather than a small number of homogeneous, large-scale solutions. Large nuclear power plants and giant dams are examples of scalable technologies that may not be sustainable if we take a genuinely systems-oriented and long-term perspective.

Just as the word "technology" will have a broader meaning for twenty-first-century cities, "infrastructure" will mean more than roads, bridges, and elaborate sewerage and flood-control systems. Again, Curitiba pioneered this principle: rather than spend millions on a flood-control infrastructure based on pipes and pumps, the city invested a much smaller sum to conserve a network of green spaces that absorb and filter floodwater while providing respite for human and nonhuman species. More broadly, urban infrastructure needs to focus primarily on ensuring that cities do not degrade the resilience of a region's natural systems. To this end, it should link urban and rural areas in ways that are beneficial to both; that is, rural areas should not just be sources and sinks for urban areas. Developing-country cities have the opportunity to design harmonious systems that connect food, water, energy, and waste. China's new city of Dongtan aims to have less than half the ecological footprint of a conventional city of comparable size—that is, it will have a dramatically smaller impact on its surroundings than a twentieth-century city. For example, according to the plans, a double-piping system will provide drinking water, as well as treated wastewater for toilets and for irrigation of vertical farms; no more than 10 percent of Dongtan's trash will end up in landfills; and all the energy consumed in the city will come from renewable sources.

Can we invent, or even design, our way out of the mess we are in? Amory Lovins has been arguing since the 1970s that the technology exists to reduce resource use (and hence the cost of production) dramatically, without sacrificing performance (see, for example, Lovins 1975). Yet change has come only gradually, suggesting that the obstacles are not technological but economic, cultural, and political. As *World Development Report 2010* observes, many of the prescriptions for climate change mitigation "have proven elusive in the past, raising the question of what might make the needed reforms and behavior changes possible" (World Bank 2009, 18–19).

How, then, can developing cities create governance systems that will address sustainability in a meaningful way? The 1990s saw a tidal wave of claims about participatory, collaborative problem solving. But the evidence suggests that convening a participatory process can be an excuse for abdication by political decision makers. Participation by local residents is essential, but equally so are leaders who can make a persuasive case for sustainability, particularly in places where there is no "culture of sustainability." Leadership and persuasion are required because a truly sustainable approach to development will involve reconceptualizing the economic system by treating the physical system as a real constraint and directing creative energies toward figuring out how to improve the quality of peoples' lives in ways that do not degrade that system. For some of us, this makes intuitive sense: just as human beings stop growing relatively early in life, spending most of their time developing, so should human societies. But a great deal of power at the local, national, and international levels is currently held by people with a fundamentally different worldview.

A second notion that gained currency in the 1990s is that we should rely exclusively on the private sector to diffuse energy conservation measures and alternative-energy technologies. But the evidence suggests that well-designed rules and incentives are much more effective than voluntary measures in precipitating behavioral change. Furthermore, government intervention is essential to ensure that the costs and benefits of change are equitably distributed. Left to themselves, markets do not move fast enough, and when they do move, the changes are abrupt and painful—and, almost invariably, most damaging to those least able to endure the harms. That said, government is often most effective when it harnesses the power of markets to serve long-term social interests.

Finally, although local leadership is critical, cities—particularly those in the developing world—will not be successful if they have to make the required transformation on their own. They need national governments to modify the context in which they operate. In particular, national governments should price natural capital in ways that reflect the social and environmental costs of extracting and using it. For example, they should ensure that energy costs reflect the environmental and social costs of extracting, transporting, and using fossil fuels. In Europe, where gasoline prices have been high for decades, carbon footprints are half those in North America. Rising gasoline prices in the United States in the spring of 2009 confirmed what ecological economists have been saying for decades: if we price resources correctly, many of the behavioral changes needed for sustainability will occur spontaneously. At the same time, to reduce inequities, governments must balance the rising costs of natural capital with lower taxes on labor.

Tensions and Challenges

A host of fundamental challenges to urban sustainability have the potential to thwart progress. First, how we will get beyond the fact that in its current form, the global economy is built on ever-increasing consumption? In *Cradle-to-Cradle*, William McDonough and Michael Braungart (2002) argue that if we create ecofriendly products, we will not need to worry about curbing consumption. Although this vision is appealing, it is not rooted in biological reality. In practice, functioning ecological systems cannot withstand infinite levels of withdrawal and conversion. In many cases, pollution is a matter of dose, not toxicity. For example, nitrogen and carbon dioxide, both of which are essential for life, become pollutants when emitted in large quantities.

Second, how will proponents of an alternative development trajectory address the objection that, for developing countries, sustainability is not the top priority? How will the world's poorest cities meet the housing needs of squatters who are currently living in ecologically vulnerable areas? Is the developed world prepared to create incentives for rapidly developing countries such as Brazil, China, and India to shift course? On this last point, a 2009 report by the Global Carbon Project shows that carbon dioxide emissions are accelerating and are close to the highest scenario considered by the Intergovernmental Panel on Climate Change (IPCC), and that more than half of global emissions are now from developing countries (GCP 2009). One important observation made in the *World Development Report* is that climate mitigation measures are almost always effective climate adaptation measures. This makes sense: truly sustainable systems are resilient in the face of changing conditions. But suspicions run deep that sustainability is a wealthy-country agenda being foisted on developing nations, and developing nations deserve a compelling explanation for why this need not be so. (Here, the mindsets of development professionals can be at least as big an obstacle as those of local officials.)

In our efforts to persuade developing (and developed) countries to pursue sustainability, we should resist the temptation to simply translate the argument for sustainability into conventional economic terms—an approach that is currently dominant in the United States. In fact, a new report issued by the Worldwatch Institute suggests that many "green" jobs will be dirty, unsafe, and poorly paid; if done on the cheap, sorting electronic wastes and other recycling and agricultural labor is dangerous work (Renner, Sweeney, and Kubit 2008). How will we ensure that developing-country cities do not become the "green" labor force for developed countries?

Finally, there is no reason to believe that identical prescriptions make sense for cities in countries at different stages of development. How will we determine which approaches to urban sustainability work best under what conditions? Fortunately, organizations such as the United Nations HABITAT Best Practices and Local Leadership Program (BLP) and Local Governments for Sustainability (ICLEI) are collecting useful information on best practices. That information, however, is no substitute for systematic evaluation of policies and practices across cities and over time. Baseline greenhouse gas inventories and metabolism studies, as well as performance-based criteria for measuring progress, are essential. Cities should continue to experiment and to share experiences and should be willing to adjust and adapt. But we also need a better understanding of how and why particular mechanisms work in specific contexts.

References

Global Carbon Project (GCP). 2009. "Carbon Budget" Web page, November 17. http://www.globalcarbonproject.org/carbonbudget/index.htm.

Lovins, Amory B. 1975. *World Energy Strategies: Facts, Issues, and Options.* San Francisco, CA: Friends of the Earth International.

McDonough, William, and Michael Braungart. 2002. *Cradle to Cradle: Remaking the Way We Make Things.* New York: North Point Press.

Renner, Michael, Sean Sweeney, and Jill Kubit. 2008. *Green Jobs: Working for People and the Environment.* Worldwatch Report 177. Washington, DC: Worldwatch Institute.

World Bank. 2009. *World Development Report 2010: Development and Climate Change.* Washington, DC: World Bank.

Promoting Research, Innovation, and Technology Transfers for Alternative Energy Sources

CLAUDIA KEMFERT

Today's society faces two main energy-related challenges: to guarantee a secure and affordable energy supply, and to reduce and eliminate environmental and climate damage caused by energy consumption. Over 80 percent of today's primary energy consumption comes from nonrenewable fossil fuels such as coal, oil, and natural gas. Without changes in behavior, the share of nonrenewable fossil fuel resources in primary energy consumption will be as high in the future as it is today, and importing countries will remain vulnerable to supply disruptions and energy price shocks. Fossil fuel consumption generates greenhouse gas emissions, leading to climate change. As the International Energy Agency (IEA) argues, the future energy mix should not be underinvested, vulnerable, and dirty, but clean, clever, and competitive.

Secure, reliable, and affordable energy resources are fundamental to sustained economic development. The risk of disruptive climate change, the erosion of energy security, and the world's growing demand for energy all pose major challenges for energy decision makers. To meet these challenges and transform our energy system, a better use of existing technologies will be required, along with significant scientific innovation to spur the adoption of new energy technologies. Additional research funding is critically needed to develop a sustainable energy future. Research priorities include photovoltaics, carbon capture and sequestration (CCS), biofuels, and hydrogen generation, storage, and use.

Today's society faces, in a way that no previous generation has, two main energy-related challenges: to guarantee a secure and affordable energy supply, and to reduce and eliminate environmental and climate damage caused by energy consumption. Over 80 percent of today's primary energy consumption comes from nonrenewable

Claudia Kemfert is professor of energy economics and sustainability at the Humboldt University of Berlin and is head of the Energy, Transportation, and Environment Department at the Deutsches Institut für Wirtschaftsforschung.

Berlin Workshop Series 2010
© 2010 The International Bank for Reconstruction and Development / The World Bank

fossil fuels such as coal, oil, and natural gas. If we do not change our behavior, the future share of fossil fuel resources will remain as high as it is today. Because few areas of the world harbor major oil and gas reserves, importing countries will be more vulnerable to supply disruptions and energy price shocks. Furthermore, fossil fuel consumption generates emissions of carbon dioxide (CO_2) and other greenhouse gases, leading to climate change. As the International Energy Agency (IEA) has emphasized in recent reports, the future energy mix should not be underinvested, vulnerable, and dirty, but clean, clever, and competitive.

Secure, reliable, and affordable energy resources are fundamental to sustained economic development. The threat of disruptive climate change, the erosion of energy security, and the world's growing demand for energy all pose major challenges for energy decision makers. To meet these challenges and transform our energy system, a better use of existing technologies will be required, along with significant scientific innovation to spur the adoption of new energy technologies. Urgent action is needed to rapidly develop and apply available energy-efficiency and low-carbon technologies and practices. Funding for basic science and energy research has been declining in the public and private sectors for the past several years. Additional funding is critically needed to develop a sustainable energy future. Research priorities encompass, among other things, photovoltaics, carbon capture and sequestration (CCS), biofuels, and hydrogen generation, storage, and use.

The Challenge

Increasing energy prices, especially for oil and gas, and recent geopolitical events such as the situation in Iran and the tension between the Russian Federation and Ukraine over natural gas have reminded us of the essential role affordable energy plays in economic growth and human development and of the vulnerability of the global energy system to disruptions in supply. Securing energy supplies is once again at the top of the international policy agenda. Yet the current pattern of energy supply carries the threat of severe and irreversible environmental damage, including changes in global climate. Reconciliation of the goals of energy security and environmental protection requires strong and coordinated government action and public support. The decoupling of energy use and economic growth, diversification of energy supply, and mitigation of climate change–causing emissions are more urgent than ever.

The greatest share of primary energy demand is being met today by fossil fuels—oil, natural gas, and coal (figure 1). The main suppliers of oil are the members of the Organization of the Petroleum Exporting Countries (OPEC), Russia, and the United States. If demand for oil continues to grow as fast as it has in recent decades, it will exceed supply 15 years from now—the depletion point. Although the price of oil would rise with increasing demand, and further exploitation of other oil reserves such as oil shale and tar sands would become financially attractive, oil still remains the scarcest fossil resource on earth, with natural gas second. Russia has the world's largest gas reserves, followed by Qatar and Iran. The supply of coal is more widespread, over many countries, and coal reserves will last more than 200 years.

FIGURE 1.
World Energy Use, by Fuel Type, 1980–2030

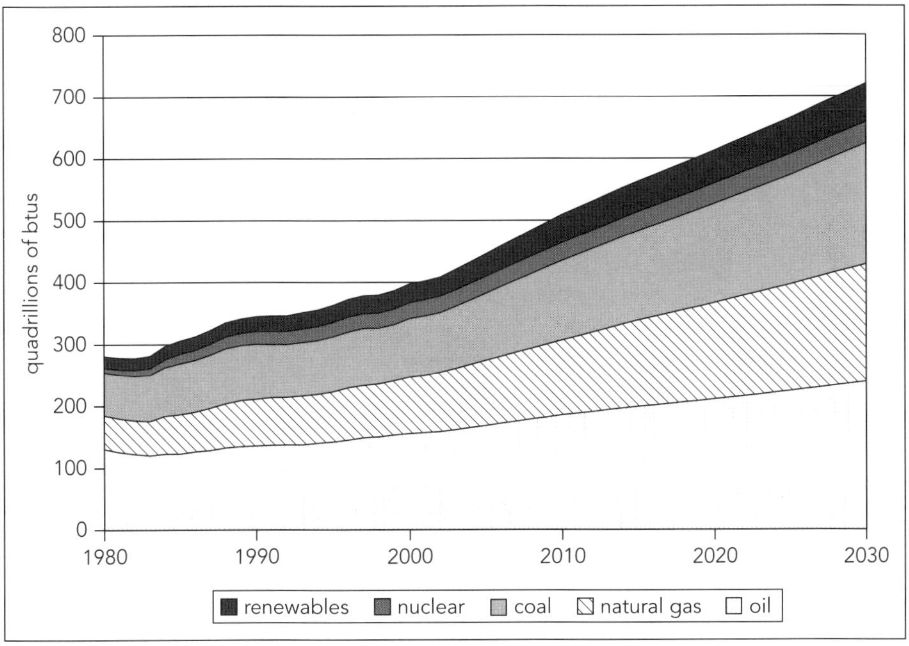

Source: EIA 2007.

Note: Btu, British thermal unit.

Energy forecasts demonstrate that the share of fossil fuels in energy supply will remain high in the absence of policies aimed at achieving a sustainable energy future (IEA 2007). The largest members of the Organisation for Economic Co-operation and Development (OECD) have successfully decoupled their energy consumption from economic growth, primarily through increased energy efficiency, but energy consumption in developing countries continues to grow rapidly (figure 2). The enormous growth of the economy and of fuel consumption in developing countries—especially in China, followed by India—will exacerbate scarcities in energy supply and will lead to higher energy prices but also to higher carbon dioxide emissions. If no sustainable policy is put in place, global energy-related carbon dioxide emissions will rise by 55 percent between 2003 and 2030. Developing countries will account for more than three-quarters of the global increase.

Because of high economic and energy consumption growth, OECD members and developing Asian countries will become increasingly dependent on imports as their indigenous production fails to keep pace with demand. By 2030, according to the projections, the OECD as a whole will import two-thirds of its oil needs, compared with 56 percent today. Much of the additional imports will come from the Middle East, along vulnerable maritime routes. The concentration of oil production in a small group of countries with large reserves—notably, Middle Eastern OPEC members and Russia—will increase these countries' market dominance and their ability to impose higher prices. An increasing share of gas demand is also expected to be met

FIGURE 2.
Carbon Dioxide Emissions, by Region, 1980–2030

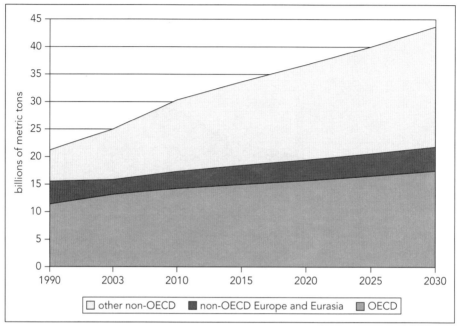

Source: EIA 2007.

Note: OECD, Organisation for Economic Co-operation and Development. A billion is 1,000 million.

by imports, via pipeline or in the form of liquefied natural gas from increasingly distant suppliers.

Meeting the world's growing hunger for energy requires massive investment in energy-supply infrastructure. The IEA forecasts cumulative investments of around US$20 trillion within the next 25 years (IEA 2005). If these investments are not made, a secure energy supply cannot be guaranteed.

A Sustainable Energy Future

A sustainable energy future must be carbon dioxide free, environmental friendly, and secure. A future energy system cannot rely on only one energy source but must be as broad as possible (figure 3). Energy security also means that energy imports are reduced and are diversified among many different supplier countries and that domestic energy sources make a major contribution. Many domestic energy sources are not sustainable; coal emits climate-harming carbon dioxide emissions, and nuclear energy carries high environmental risks. Conventional nuclear energy can only serve as a technology to bridge the gap between the fossil fuel and carbon-free technology eras. Three main pillars can contribute to a sustainable energy future:

1. *Energy efficiency.* Economic growth and growth of energy consumption need to be decoupled. Many developed nations, including European countries and Japan, have

FIGURE 3.
Future Energy Technology Mix

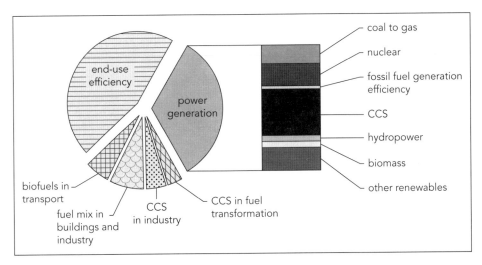

Source: IEA 2006a.

Note: CCS, carbon capture and sequestration.

been quite successful in this respect. Others, such as the United States, can improve or, like China and India, need to start soon. Global energy consumption and emissions can be reduced by 24 percent by 2050 only through energy-efficiency measures.

2. *An increased share of renewable energy* in electricity production, as alternative fuels, and for heating. The use of renewable energy in electricity production could be increased from 5 to 16 percent globally, and the share of biofuels can be drastically increased, up to 10 percent globally (IEA 2006a).

3. *Carbon capture and sequestration (CCS).* Coal power plants can be made more environmentally friendly ("CO_2-low power plant") by capturing and storing carbon dioxide emissions, but the environmental and financial risks have not yet been sufficiently explored. If CCS technology is available in the future, production costs may double (IEA 2005; IPCC 2005).

The main aim is to make future energy systems sustainable by, on the one hand, increasing energy efficiency and, on the other hand, establishing innovative, carbon-free, and environmentally friendly technologies. In 100 years the share of renewable energy could increase up to 80 percent. In the interim, carbon capture and storage technology can play a dominant role.

Research Agenda for a Sustainable Energy Future

Funding for basic science and energy research has been declining in the public and private sectors for the past several years. Additional funding is critically needed to develop a sustainable energy future. Although public funding has remained almost stable in

FIGURE 4.
Public R&D Expenditures for Energy Research, Germany, Japan, and the United States, 1990–2007

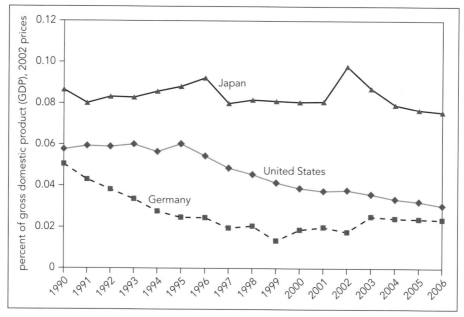

Source: AAAS 2006; BMW 2007.

Note: R&D, research and development. Data for the United States omit defense.

Germany and Japan, the overall level of research and development (R&D) spending for energy research is far too low (figure 4). Research needs are briefly outlined below.

1. *Governance: Double R&D energy expenditures and strengthen national, European, and international cooperation.* Public, as well as private, R&D expenditures should be doubled in order to explore all the risks and opportunities involved in a path toward a sustainable energy system. It is important to mobilize national and European funding and to explore new options for launching large, integrated projects, such as joint initiatives for innovative technologies. Further international cooperation would be desirable, especially with emerging countries such as China and India.

2. *Competitiveness: Strengthen and accelerate R&D priorities to support strategic deployment.* Promotion of innovative technologies for a sustainable energy future enables new branches and sectors to grow and to become more competitive. Especially because a strengthening of renewable energy improves the competitiveness of small business firms, fostering renewable energy creates growth machines and increases competitiveness.

3. *Technologies and products: reduction of uncertainty.* Innovation for a sustainable energy system requires technology breakthroughs and less uncertainty. Some examples of priorities in this area follow:

- *Energy storage.* In compressed air energy storage (CAES), off-peak electricity is used to power a motor or generator that drives compressors to force air into an underground storage reservoir. This process typically occurs when utility system demands and electricity costs are lowest. More research is necessary in order to explore other energy storage types and assess the environmental and financial risks.

- *Low-cost photovoltaics: reduction of solar energy costs through biotechnology and nanotechnology.* A decrease in the cost of installed photovoltaic systems to competitive levels will require technologies that do not exist at present, including approaches that yield ultrahigh conversion efficiency at modest cost, hybrid conversion materials, and nanostructured materials (materials at a size between molecular and microscopic scales that offer substantial efficiency gains in solar energy conversion).

- *Biofuels and other advanced fuels.* Biomass is an abundant renewable resource that has the potential to make a substantial difference in liquid fuel supply. Overall product yields and productivity must be improved, however. Emerging knowledge in genomics and molecular technologies provides new opportunities for the genetic tailoring of plants and microorganisms to produce novel materials, fuels, and chemicals. Cofiring of biomass may be an attractive option for power plants, as carbon dioxide precombustion technology is very similar to that used to produce synthetic gas from biomass.

- *Carbon-free hydrogen generation, storage, and use.* One method currently used for hydrogen production is steam reforming of natural gas. In the future, other production technologies that are more efficient and that use more sustainable feedstocks will be required. Processes that hold promise include gasification of biomass or organic wastes, electrolysis of water using electricity from renewable sources, and nuclear power. Lack of practical storage methods has hindered the widespread use of hydrogen fuels. Researchers are advancing a new class of compounds known as hydrogen clathrates, as well as carbon nanotubes.

- *Reduction of the costs and risks of carbon capture and storage.* Today, carbon dioxide is already being captured at a handful of electricity generation, manufacturing, and fuel-processing plants and is being stored in saline aquifers or injected into oil and gas fields to enhance recovery. Several important scientific research areas, including use of advanced membranes to separate and capture carbon dioxide and more sophisticated methods of identifying and monitoring storage reservoirs, need to be pushed in order to successfully exploit the promise of sustainable capture and storage of carbon dioxide.

- *Advanced fission and fusion.* The development of future fusion power plants will face similar development issues as will the future generation of fission plants in achieving the goals of technical feasibility and operability. Except for plasma physics, the principal challenges for fusion reactors are in the areas of materials development for the heat source structures (plasma facing material for fusion, and materials for the fission core) and the design of cooling systems for high efficiencies.

Summary

A sustainable energy future must be carbon dioxide free, environmentally friendly, and secure. A future energy system cannot rely on only one energy source but must be as broad as possible. Energy security also means that energy imports are reduced and are diversified among many different supplier countries and that domestic energy sources make a major contribution. Many domestic energy sources are not sustainable; coal emits climate-harming carbon dioxide emissions, and nuclear energy carries high environmental risks. Conventional nuclear energy can therefore serve only as a technology that bridges the gap between the fossil fuel and carbon-free technology eras. The main aim is to make future energy systems sustainable by, on the one hand, increasing energy efficiency and, on the other hand, establishing innovative, carbon-free, and environmentally friendly technologies. In 100 years, the share of renewable energy could increase up to 80 percent. In the interim, carbon capture and storage technology can play a dominant role.

References

AAAS (American Association for the Advancement of Science). 2006. "AAAS Report XXXI: Research and Development FY 2007." AAAS, Washington, DC. http://www.aaas.org/spp/rd/rd07main.htm.

BMW (Bundesministerium für Wirtschaft und Technologie). 2007. *Energiestatistik*. Berlin: BMW.

EIA (U.S. Energy Information Administration). 2007. "World Carbon Emissions." EIA, Washington, DC.

IEA (International Energy Agency). 2005. "Reducing Greenhouse Gas Emissions: The Potential of Coal." IEA, Paris. http://www.iea.org/publications/free_new_Desc.asp?PUBS_ID=1478.

———. 2006a. *Energy Technology Perspectives: Scenarios and Strategies to 2050*. Paris: Organisation for Economic Co-operation and Development (OECD).

———. 2006b. "Science for Today's Energy Challenges: Accelerating Progress for a Sustainable Energy Future." IEA, Paris. http://www.iea.org/publications/free_new_Desc.asp?PUBS_ID=1846.

———. 2007. *World Energy Outlook 2007*. Paris: Organisation for Economic Co-operation and Development (OECD) Publishing. http://www.iea.org/textbase/nppdf/free/2007/weo_2007.pdf.

IPCC (Intergovernmental Panel on Climate Change). 2005. *Special Report on Carbon Dioxide Capture and Storage*. Cambridge, U.K.: Cambridge University Press.

Part III
Natural Resource Governance for Adaptation, Mitigation, and Development

Governance for Sustainable Adaptation? Environmental Stressors, Natural Resources, and Human Security

SIRI ERIKSEN

In addition to strengthening institutional frameworks, governance for adaptation entails addressing existing power structures and the politics inherent in the adaptation process. Interventions or governance systems that focus on only one stressor or that assume homogeneity in a group can inadvertently increase exposure to stressors and reduce response capacity. Governance systems need to approach vulnerability and adaptation more holistically. This entails being able to grasp the diverse reasons for vulnerability within a heterogeneous group, even at a local level, and having the capacity and maneuvering space to develop cross-sectoral and sometimes "nonenvironmental" interventions. Putting adaptation and vulnerable groups first entails a reprioritization that has political ramifications and potentially involves challenging prevailing development discourses and governance systems. Among the central issues are how institutions, rules, and regulations are set up to ensure various rights, such as labor rights, and whose interests are promoted in the operation of institutional and legal frameworks. Building on principles of sustainable adaptation, with a focus on equity and environmental integrity, is one way of achieving governance for adaptation.

This paper discusses the challenges that governance for adaptation must address in order to ensure human security in the face of multiple stressors, including climate change. Examples are drawn from past studies of natural resource–dependent societies in Africa. Human security exists when and where individuals and communities have the options necessary to end, mitigate, or adapt to threats to their human, environmental, and social rights, possess the capacity and freedom to exercise these

Siri Eriksen is an associate professor at the Department of International Development and Environment Studies, Norwegian University of Life Sciences, Aas, Norway. The author thanks Frank Sperling, WWF Norway, for helpful comments on an earlier draft of this paper.

Berlin Workshop Series 2010

options, and actively participate in attaining these options (GECHS 1999). There is growing awareness of the importance of social organization and the operation of institutions in governing adaptation actions. Governance—the decisions, actors, processes, institutional structures, mechanisms, division of authority, and underlying norms involved in determining a course of action—is important both for how individuals, households, and local communities adapt and for the adaptive capacity of institutions themselves in the face of climate change (Adger 2000; Ivey et al. 2004; Adger, Lorenzoni, and O'Brien 2009; Keskitalo and Kulyasova 2009). Features of governance such as technical and financial capacity, institutional memory and learning, and participation, empowerment, and accountability have been proposed as conducive to adaptation, although so far very few empirical studies of governance for adaptation exist (Eakin et al. 2009).

This paper argues that, in addition to, or cutting across, these key features of governance for adaptation, existing power structures and the politics inherent in the adaptation process must be addressed. Governance for adaptation and development is not just a matter of adjusting existing governance systems or establishing institutional frameworks that facilitate practices in, for example, farming, which are well adjusted to climatic change or uncertainty; it is also a question of ensuring that the most vulnerable have access to means of securing well-being, as well as control over their own life situations. Studies of environmental governance and resilience have pointed out that simply decentralizing natural resource management to the local level without addressing existing power structures can reproduce social inequities (Nelson, Adger, and Brown 2007). A human security perspective on climate change draws attention to people as active agents in responding to change, underlining that their options and ability to do so are highly differentiated and that vulnerability is interlinked across geographic contexts through social and environmental transformation processes (O'Brien 2006). In the next section, the ways in which local vulnerability and responses may be affected differentially by governance structures and related adaptation interventions and by the ability of actors to negotiate those outcomes are described. The paper concludes that building on principles of sustainable adaptation which focus on equity and environmental integrity is one way of achieving governance for adaptation. This may imply shifting development discourses and changing governance systems altogether.

Features of Local Vulnerability

We focus on three key characteristics of local vulnerability that have implications for governance for adaptation. First, people's responses to climate change are embedded in a context of multiple stressors. Second, the vulnerability context is highly differentiated, geographically and socially. Third, people's responses to multiple shocks and changes are intrinsically political processes.

Feature 1: A Context of Multiple Stressors

Responses to climate change take place in a context of multiple stressors—that is, social and environmental processes of change, in the form of either gradual transformations or sudden shocks. Stressors such as drought, floods, changing seasonality, biodiversity loss, changes in rules and regulations, economic liberalization, conflict, and the spread of HIV/AIDS interact with people's capacity to respond to generate the vulnerability context (O'Brien, Quinlan, and Ziervogel 2009). People strive to adapt to risks to their human, environmental, and social rights by accessing the options, material or nonmaterial, available to them. Viewing climate change as a human security issue means that environmental change is understood as occurring within a wider context of concurrent economic, social, institutional, political, cultural, and economic changes taking place in the world (O'Brien 2006). For example, huge transformations—land tenure change, conflicts, political change, and altered labor markets—are currently occurring in southern Africa (Eriksen and Watson 2009).

These transformations make governance for adaptation a political issue because they mean that the drivers of vulnerability are not confined to natural resources or to particular sectors, institutions, or local communities but are, rather, societywide and multisectoral in scope. Changes in one sector, group, or geographic area have effects on the vulnerability of others. Governing adaptation means negotiating competing, and sometimes conflicting, interests. Even pastoralist or farmer systems that are well adjusted to climatic stressors, such as uncertainty of rainfall, may be vulnerable. This is because vulnerability is not a matter of climatic factors alone but stems from a multiplicity of risks that people experience, including market risks, bad health, poor infrastructure, and loss of pasture. Moreover, households do not make a living exclusively from one activity, such as farming or livestock keeping, but, instead, operate in multiple economic sectors and geographic locations—for example by collecting forest products, fishing, drawing on social networks, engaging in local employment, and sharing in urban incomes (Eriksen, Brown, and Kelly 2005; Ziervogel, Bharwani, and Downing 2006; Tschakert 2007).

The processes that create risks to any of these activities, including economic, policy, and legal changes, often take place outside the realm of a rural community. Local systems of natural resource use can be sensitive to such pressures from outside because they alter the viability of existing livelihood activities and the power and operation of existing institutions (Benjaminsen et al. 2006; Eriksen and Lind 2009). These pressures form part of the multiple stressors that shape the vulnerability context. Liberalization of trade and privatization of land tenure, for example, affect factors critical to response capacity. A study in Mozambique found that the unintended effects on vulnerable households include reduced availability of household labor, concentration of capital availability in a few households, declines in formal employment opportunities, and increased competition from commercial interests in accessing land and natural resources (Eriksen and Silva 2009).

Addressing the causes of vulnerability may involve discerning competing interests in societal change and challenging both prevailing development discourses and the existing power relations that frame decision making. In southern Africa, policy outcomes have often favored commercial farmers over smallholders in matters of access to land, agricultural support services, and markets (Bowen, Chilundo, and Tique 2003; Benjaminsen et al. 2006; Clover and Eriksen 2009). These inequities are particularly worrying when, in a setting of commercialization and privatization of resources, populations lose rights to nonmonetary natural resources that serve as a safety net in facing increased climate variability. Such resources include grazing areas, wild foods, and forest products, which are critical for the most vulnerable populations in surviving droughts (Eriksen, Brown, and Kelly 2005).

The wide scope of the socioecological changes to which people respond means that sources of vulnerability link across space—for example, between urban and rural areas and across international borders—as well as across sectors. These interactions influence capacity to respond to climate-related events and changes. To illustrate, the loss of urban industrial employment means that remittances to rural households become more unreliable. This has important repercussions on livelihood diversification because remittances are often the most important source of investment for livestock raising, business, or other activities. Similarly, the increased unemployment in South Africa and the related reduced labor immigration to South Africa from neighboring countries means that households in Mozambique, for example, increasingly turn to informal migration and unreliable, poorly paid jobs (Eriksen and Silva 2009). In practice, many households lose labor power when a family member leaves, without getting remittances in return. They thus lose a source of income that in the past ensured basic needs in times when harvests or rural livelihood sources failed.

The ramifications of changes in one sector can be wide because the income from one activity such as livestock is invested in another. For example, the loss of health associated with the spread of infectious diseases means that farming and other economic activities, as well as domestic tasks, suffer; social support networks are strained; and families break up. Governance for adaptation therefore entails altering the governance system so that it can address the processes that create vulnerability holistically and across scales, rather than targeting the operation of individual sectors and their related institutions separately. Governance systems are required that can deal with co-occurring environmental, economic, social, institutional, political, cultural, and economic processes in such a way that adaptation and, in particular, the interests of vulnerable groups come first. This may involve a totally different approach to development reforms, land tenure changes, and the way in which processes such as urbanization and migration are tackled. Such a reprioritization has both institutional and political ramifications. For example, disaster management and relief have traditionally been managed by civil defense–type institutions, and climate change by environmental departments (Sperling and Szekely 2005), but a more holistic and cross-sectoral approach to adaptation can only be accommodated if adaptation becomes a central and formalized concern of development ministries.

Feature 2: A Highly Differentiated Vulnerability Context

The interaction between stressors and response capacity makes up the vulnerability context, which varies greatly from place to place, between individuals, and over time. The transformations described above affect people differentially, and so their outcomes raise questions concerning equity, justice, power relations, and whose security is prioritized by the way that society responds to the changes through its governance systems. Some people are particularly badly hit by multiple stressors, such as the interaction between economic liberalization or the spread of HIV/AIDS and climate change (Leichenko and O'Brien 2008; O'Brien, Quinlan, and Ziervogel 2009).

This differentiation has several implications for adaptation interventions and the way they are framed by governance systems. First, groups are not homogeneous, either in their levels of vulnerability or in the causes of their vulnerability. Hidden and unexpected sources of vulnerability may exist, and so, for example, a measure to formalize markets that reduces the vulnerability of some urban traders may actually increase the vulnerability of other urban traders (O'Brien, Quinlan, and Ziervogel 2009). Furthermore, vulnerability and poverty are not the same. Poor people may be vulnerable in very diverse ways; they may vary in their responses to change (Coetzee 2002); and they therefore may be very differently affected by governance systems. In addition, the relatively less poor can sometimes be more vulnerable than the poor— for example, if they are locked into dependence on climate-sensitive crops with high market fluctuations and do not have the flexibility to diversify (Eakin 2006; Ziervogel, Bharwani, and Downing 2006). Interventions or governance systems that focus on only one stressor or that assume homogeneity in a group can inadvertently increase exposure to stressors and reduce response capacity.

Eriksen and Lind (2009) study this heterogeneity in a dryland area in eastern Kenya. Here, pastoralists require access to water and grazing during droughts. Trade in livestock and household goods and the renting out of wells and grazing land to pastoralists have become principal drought incomes for some agropastoralists. At the same time, the renting out of wells to wealthy pastoralists can impede the currently free access to wells by poor agropastoralists. The group of poor agropastoralists is, however, also heterogeneous. Even though many feel that their drought-period access to water is threatened by pastoralists' presence, some of the poor people profit from engaging in trade with the pastoralists. In addition, some of the most vulnerable (in terms of their ability to control their own life situations) include relatively wealthy pastoralists: their access to wells and trade, which is critical for their ability to adapt to protracted drought, is at the mercy of decisions by local politicians and administrations that primarily represent agropastoralist interests. In other words, the pastoralists have little say in political processes, policy development, or natural resource management systems that determine their ability to ensure their own well-being in the face of socioenvironmental changes. In this case, climate adaptation interventions based on single-stressor understanding, such as water provision for irrigated farming or fenced ranching, could benefit a few people but would at the same time hinder access to water and trade and increase vulnerability among both pastoralists and agropastoralists.

Governance systems clearly need to be able to grasp the diverse reasons for vulnerability among a heterogeneous group, even at a local level. This entails having the capacity and maneuvering space to develop cross-sectoral and sometimes "nonenvironmental" interventions, such as the strengthening of conflict resolution mechanisms to facilitate trade, *as well as* confront inequities in water and land rights to ensure that the poor have access to water in time of drought. A governance system that allows for highly diverse and very localized measures for reducing vulnerability may require the decentralization of decisions and development funding to local levels and the empowerment of local institutions in order to create what Thomas and Twyman (2005) term "headroom" within which local actions can develop. Allowing for diverse knowledge systems and local knowledge will be important in such a process of empowerment.

Feature 3: Political Dimensions of Responses to Multiple Shocks and Changes

Since vulnerability and decision-making power are highly differentiated socially, even within a village, decentralization and empowerment of local institutions alone do not ensure that the human security of the most vulnerable is strengthened. As the case above demonstrates, local adaptation involves a continuous negotiation of competing interests between groups. Since one person's adaptation strategy may increase someone else's vulnerability, or a government adaptation intervention aimed at one group may disadvantage another, adaptation is an intrinsically political issue. In the Kenyan case, those in favor of and those opposed to agropastoralist-pastoralist trade competed for influence with the local and district administrations to sway decisions toward either allowing or banning trade and pastoralist presence. Climate-related stressors such as drought, and strategies for responding to them, including trade, can also alter existing power structures. Since trade and the renting out of wells yielded an increasing economic income and created new groups of economically influential people, competition for political influence actually became part of the adaptation process in the Kenyan case (Eriksen and Lind 2009).

Negotiation of competing interests is part of the adaptation process. It takes place not only directly between villagers and groups but also as people respond to social transformations and government policies—that is, as they seek relations of influence with changing societal structures such as labor and agricultural markets. As mentioned earlier, policy attention and investments are often skewed toward commercial farmers and large landowners at the expense of small-scale resource users. Many populations in southern Africa, for example, have a poor negotiating position in labor and trade markets that locks them into unreliable and short-term survival-type strategies at the expense of long-term livelihood security and capacity to respond to future change such as climatic change (Eriksen and Watson 2009). Commercial actors are often more powerful in getting their interests promoted by means of policies. Inequity in the pattern of land access, in economic and social support, and in access to markets, capital, and labor have been compounded by a shift in the focus of land reform from reduction of poverty to privatization of land and economic efficiency (Clover and Eriksen 2009). In Namibia decentralization and cost recovery in water supply were found to cause marginalization, and in Botswana poorer populations were excluded from access to rural support programs because they could not afford the required investments (Thomas and Twyman 2005). These patterns are making agricultural livelihoods economically unsustainable for the majority of small-holders, while threatening equity and social justice and contributing to poverty (Thomas and Twyman 2005). Central issues for governance here are how institutions, rules, and regulations are set up to ensure different rights, such as labor rights, and whose interests are promoted in the operation of institutional and legal frameworks. Thomas and Twyman (2005) argue that in addition to decentralization, the place of equity in outcomes needs to become a primary concern.

Implications for Governance

The above features of vulnerability imply several challenges with respect to how governance can facilitate adaptation. The first issue central to human security that governance must address is people's access to the means of ensuring their well-being—access to social infrastructure, cultural rights, employment, economic activities such as farming, natural resources, and so on. In addition to ensuring people access to the means of responding to change, however, governance systems must also strengthen the ability of vulnerable populations to influence political processes, policy development, economic changes, and natural resource management systems and hence ensure their adaptation interests. The importance of this second aspect is demonstrated by the vulnerability of pastoralists in the Kenyan case. Where both access to means of securing well-being and ability to negotiate with competing interests are in place, people are likely to have greater human security and be less vulnerable to climate change.

Governance for adaptation must acknowledge that not all adaptation interventions or institutional structures are necessarily benign for everyone. It is essential to identify the potential unintended detrimental effects on vulnerable people of an institutional structure or intervention. One way of doing this is for governance to be based on principles of sustainable adaptation—adaptation that addresses inequity and poverty but avoids endangering future environmental integrity by, for example, causing increased greenhouse gas emissions or biodiversity loss (Eriksen and O'Brien 2007). In order to address inequity, governance must prioritize outcomes that reduce risks to current ways of securing well-being, strengthen the adaptive capacity of the poor, and address the causes of vulnerability of the poor. Table 1 outlines the measures that such a three-pronged approach may involve. Importantly, a single measure on its own does not constitute sustainable adaptation. Instead, a whole set of measures that are appropriate for a specific context—in terms of simultaneously targeting climate risk, strengthening adaptive capacity, and addressing the causes of vulnerability—may together effectively contribute to sustainable adaptation. The table hence only exemplifies the general types of factors related to vulnerability among the poor and the potential measures that may be relevant for a given context. Ulsrud, Sygna, and O'Brien (2008) further explore the implications of such measures for practical development projects, using case studies of Ethiopia, Nepal, and Nicaragua.

TABLE 1. Examples of Actions That May Contribute to Sustainable Adaptation

Factors related to vulnerability among the poor	Adaptation measure
Climate risk	*Reduce climate risk*
Threat to lives and incomes from flood, droughts, heat waves, and cyclones in rural and urban areas	Improve early warning and evacuation procedures
Detrimental effects on agricultural production from climate variability and change	Introduce national agricultural insurance schemes Promote planting of windbreaks and crop diversification
Glacier melting, floods, and droughts threatening the water supply of the poor	Promote water conservation and construction of wells
Interruption of energy supply	Improve local renewable energy options
Damage to infrastructure and diminished access to social infrastructure	Make physical infrastructure and housing more climate resilient
Unsanitary conditions during flood and drought; spread of disease	Strengthen health and education facilities and improve their accessibility for the poor
Reduced school attendance	Adjust timing of school fee payment
Factors important for adaptive capacity of the poor	*Strengthen adaptive capacity*
Multiactivity and multilocality	Strengthen multiple economic sectors in which the poor engage Enable migration and movement across frontiers
Migration with cattle to access diverse grazing areas	Improve services along livestock migration routes Ensure rights to drought-period grazing areas
Adjustment of crop types	Promote conservation of and research on local strains and crop types
Social networks and informal income options	Ensure equitable access to key adaptation resources such as water Invest in and support local adaptation strategies
Construction of drought-period water sources and small-scale irrigation	Strengthen on-farm planting of indigenous trees and enhance flexible drought-period access to forests
Use of forest products	Improve value adding and processing of local forest products
Processes causing vulnerability	*Address causes of vulnerability*
Deagrarianization and declining profitability of agriculture	Enhance status of and investment in small-scale agriculture
Marginalization of nonfarm incomes	Legalize and regulate nonfarm drought-period incomes such as charcoal production Remove restrictions on the urban informal sector
Reduced formal employment options	Address structures making for unequal access to resources, barriers to poor people's access to formal nonfarm income opportunities, gender inequality
Economic globalization	Improve marketing channels and pricing of local products; facilitate local trade
Spread of HIV/AIDS	Strengthen health and education services; target HIV/AIDS

TABLE 1. (*Continued*)

Processes causing vulnerability (cont.)	Address causes of vulnerability (cont.)
Environmental degradation, reinforced by climate change	Mitigate environmental change Foster enhanced local participation in natural resource management
Disempowerment	Promote democratic participation in development Bring together formal and informal regulatory systems in urban planning Strengthen collective management of natural resources important for local adaptation strategies
Conflict and political processes	Strengthen peace committees, civil society, and local democratic control over development funds Strengthen social welfare programs for the destitute

Source: Adapted from Eriksen and O'Brien 2007.

A focus on equity and on the vulnerability of the poor demands that poverty alleviation and empowerment of the poor be closely related to adaptation, but the concept of human security underscores that they are nevertheless distinct. Adaptation in a human security perspective entails strengthening people's options needed to end, mitigate, or adapt to threats to their rights, as well as their ability to participate actively in attaining these options. The focus is on active responses by people and on the interconnections that create risks, that constrain people's options, and that affect their ability to negotiate access to such options. Governance for adaptation has to target the causes of vulnerability, some of which concern general marginalization but many of which originate from locally specific processes. These processes may sometimes resemble but may at other times be very different from those that create poverty. A lack of human security may, in turn, often lead to poverty, whether defined in strict material terms or more broadly.

The incorporation of principles of sustainable adaptation into governance systems has several implications. Figure 1 illustrates some of the main governance challenges in the context of the three features of vulnerability outlined above—technical and financial capacity; institutional memory and learning; and participation, empowerment, and accountability. The figure indicates the levels of governance at which the challenges may be most pressing, but it should be noted that a particular challenge often requires related governance changes at several levels and that a graphic cannot describe the relations between such governance levels in detail. An important point is that, although local human security is the main focus of this paper, the local (village or municipality), regional (district or province), and national levels are all influenced by governance at the global level—for example, through global institutions such as climate change and development institutions and through global transformations such as economic globalization. Global processes are therefore included in figure 1, even though they are not the explicit focus of this paper. The figure reflects the need for a shift in governance systems from ones in which sectoral issues or climate risks are addressed separately (through, for example, disaster response measures,

FIGURE 1.
Main Governance Challenges with Respect to Vulnerability, by Political Level

Feature of governance	Level of governance			
	Local	Regional	National	Global
Technical and financial capacity			Accommodate local vulnerability concerns and multiple stressors in adaptation funding mechanisms	
			Reduce sectoralization of climate change issues within governments and development organizations	
	Enable multisectoral, "nonenvironmental" types of vulnerability interventions			
			Integrate equity and vulnerability concerns into implementation of reforms such as privatization of services	
Institutional memory and learning	Integrate analysis of the risk, vulnerability, and equity outcomes of interventions, legal frameworks, and policies			
			Challenge dominant development ideologies that undermine equity and environmental integrity–type reforms	
	Exchange formal and informal knowledge in decision-making processes			
	Strengthen information networks and coproduction of local and formal knowledge			
Participation, empowerment, and accountability			Strengthen local participation in formulation of adaptation policy	
			Enhance rights of small-scale natural resource users in legal frameworks	
	Address inequity in land distribution and in access to water, forests, and other natural resources			
	Incorporate into legal frameworks local access and management of natural resources critical to local strategies for managing climatic variation			
	Strengthen political rights and local democratic processes that enhance the ability of vulnerable populations to influence political and economic decision-making processes			
	Strengthen local markets and trade infrastructure			
	Strengthen market systems and support for local niche products			
			Enhance conditions and rights of rural laborers, informal sector workers, immigrants, and urban workers	

Source: Author's elaboration.

flood defenses, and changes in crops and technologies) to systems that enable a multisectoral approach and allow interventions that are locally differentiated according to the vulnerability context.

Changing governance to build equity and environmental considerations into the system may be a political issue. For example, in order to address the way that New Public Management reforms in public administration in Mexico and Norway are undermining adaptive capacity (Eakin et al. 2009), or the way land reform is exacerbating vulnerability in southern Africa (Clover and Eriksen 2009), the neoliberal ideologies underpinning such reforms may have to be challenged. Some of the measures implied by a sustainable adaptation focus—such as prioritizing, within policy interventions, vulnerable populations, the natural resources they use, and their economic niches, or ensuring economic and political empowerment that shifts the bias from commercial to small-scale natural resource users—may require political reorientation and negotiations. Governance change may thus involve the challenging of existing power structures and development discourses. It is likely, for example, that many strong actors would resist attempts to strengthen local rights to nonmonetized forest resources or to regulate employment conditions and organize market outlets for niche produce to reinforce the negotiating position of rural households in trade and employment relations.

Governance for sustainable adaptation entails the politicization of the governance features conducive to adaptive capacity—technical and financial capacity; institutional memory and learning; and participation, empowerment, and accountability. Simply strengthening these three features without considering whose capacity or influence is favored over others is not enough. Instead, the governance system must be critical and must continuously ask, in whom technical and financial capacity is vested, whose knowledge is represented in learning processes, and who is empowered to promote which particular interests.

References

Adger, W. Neil. 2000. "Institutional Adaptation to Environmental Risk under the Transition in Vietnam." *Annals of the Association of American Geographers* 90 (4): 738–58.

Adger, W. Neil, Irene Lorenzoni, and Karen L. O'Brien, eds. 2009. *Adapting to Climate Change: Thresholds, Values, Governance.* Cambridge, U.K.: Cambridge University Press.

Benjaminsen, Tor A., Rick Rohde, Espen Sjaastad, Poul Wisborg, and Tom Lebert. 2006. "Land Reform, Range Ecology, and Carrying Capacities in Namaqualand, South Africa." *Annals of the Association of American Geographers* 96 (3): 524–40.

Bowen, Merle L., Alrindo Chilundo, and Cesar A. Tique. 2003. "Social Differentiation, Farming Practices and Environmental Change in Mozambique." In *African Savannas: Global Narratives and Local Knowledge of Environmental Change*, ed. Thomas J. Bassey and Donald Crummey, 225–47. Oxford, U.K.: James Currey.

Clover, J., and S. Eriksen. 2009. "The Effects of Land Tenure Change on Sustainability: Human Security and Environmental Change in Southern African Savannas." *Environmental Science and Policy* 12 (1): 53–70.

Coetzee, Erika. 2002. "Urban Vulnerability: A Conceptual Framework." In *Urban Vulnerability: Perspectives from Southern Africa*, ed. Christina Nomdo and Erika Coetzee, 2–27. Cape Town, South Africa: Periperi Publications.

Eakin, Hallie. 2006. *Weathering Risk in Rural Mexico: Climatic, Institutional, and Economic Change.* Tucson: University of Arizona Press.

Eakin, Hallie, Siri Eriksen, P. O. Eikeland, and C. R. Øyen. 2009. "Public Sector Reform and Governance for Adaptation: Implications of New Public Management for Adaptive Capacity in Mexico and Norway." Presented at the International Human Dimensions Programme on Global Environmental Change (IHDP) Open Meeting, Bonn, Germany, April 26–30.

Eriksen, Siri, and Jeremy Lind. 2009. "Adaptation as a Political Process: Adjusting to Drought and Conflict in Kenya's Drylands." *Environmental Management* 43 (5, May): 817–35.

Eriksen, Siri, and Karen O'Brien. 2007. "Vulnerability, Poverty and the Need for Sustainable Adaptation Measures." *Climate Policy* 7: 337–52.

Eriksen, Siri, and Julie A. Silva. 2009. "The Impact of Economic Liberalisation on Climate Vulnerability among Farmers in Mozambique." *Environmental Science and Policy* 12 (1): 33–52.

Eriksen, Siri, and H. K. Watson. 2009. "The Dynamic Context of Southern African Savannas: Investigating Emerging Threats and Opportunities to Sustainability." *Environmental Science and Policy* 12 (1): 5–22.

Eriksen, Siri H., Katrina Brown, and P. Mick Kelly. 2005. "The Dynamics of Vulnerability: Locating Coping Strategies in Kenya and Tanzania." *Geographical Journal* 171 (4): 287–305.

GECHS (Global Environmental Change and Human Security). 1999. *GECHS Science Plan.* International Human Dimensions Programme on Global Environmental Change (IHDP), Bonn, Germany.

Ivey, Janet L., John Smithers, Rob C. de Loe, and Reid D. Kreutzwiser. 2004. "Community Capacity for Adaptation to Climate-Induced Water Shortages: Linking Institutional Complexity and Local Actors." *Environmental Management* 33 (1): 36–47.

Keskitalo, E. Carina H., and Antonina A. Kulyasova. 2009. "The Role of Governance in Community Adaptation to Climate Change." *Polar Research* 28 (1): 60–70.

Leichenko, Robin, and Karen O'Brien. 2008. *Environmental Change and Globalization: Double Exposures.* Oxford, U.K.: Oxford University Press.

Nelson, Donald R., W. Neil Adger, and Katrina Brown. 2007. "Adaptation to Environmental Change: Contributions of a Resilience Framework." *Annual Review of Environment and Resources* 32 (1): 395–419.

O'Brien, Karen. 2006. "Are We Missing the Point? Global Environmental Change as an Issue of Human Security." *Global Environmental Change* 16 (1): 1–3.

O'Brien, Karen, T. Quinlan, and G. Ziervogel. 2009. "Assessing Vulnerability in the Context of Multiple Stressors: The Southern Africa Vulnerability Initiative (SAVI)." *Environmental Science and Policy* 12 (1): 23–32.

Sperling, Frank, and F. Szekely. 2005. "Disaster Risk Management in a Changing Climate." Discussion Paper, Vulnerability and Adaptation Resource Group (VARG), Washington, DC. http://www.adaptationlearning.net/sites/default/files/VARG%20-%20Disaster%20Risk%20Management%20in%20a%20Changing%20Climate.pdf.

Thomas, David S. G., and Chasca Twyman. 2005. "Equity and Justice in Climate Change Adaptation amongst Natural-Resource Dependent Societies." *Global Environmental Change* 15 (2): 115–24.

Tschakert, Petra. 2007. "Views from the Vulnerable: Understanding Climatic and Other Stressors in the Sahel." *Global Environmental Change* 17 (3–4): 381–96.

Ulsrud, Kirsten, Linda Sygna, and Karen O'Brien. 2008. "More Than Rain: Identifying Sustainable Pathways for Climate Adaptation and Poverty Reduction." Global Environmental Change and Human Security (GECHS)/The Development Fund, Oslo.

Ziervogel, Gina, Sukaina Bharwani, and Thomas E. Downing. 2006. "Adapting To Climate Variability: Pumpkins, People and Policy." *Natural Resources Forum* 30 (4, November): 294–305.

Impact of Climate and Land-Use Changes on Natural Resources in the Agricultural Landscape

ANDRZEJ KĘDZIORA AND ZBIGNIEW W. KUNDZEWICZ

Apart from solar and orbital forcings, global climate conditions are created and determined mainly by three sets of factors: the physical processes and properties of the atmosphere; the chemical processes and composition of the atmosphere; and the properties of and processes at the Earth's surface. All three are influenced by human activity, and this has been especially true during the last century. Three processes— energy flows, cycling of matter, and global atmospheric circulation—are primarily responsible for the functioning of the climate system on different scales. The interaction between the atmosphere and the Earth's surface influences the effect of these three processes.

Agriculture will have to feed increasing human populations in the decades to come. Yet even now, many people suffer hunger or are undernourished, and it will be difficult to achieve the United Nations Millennium Development Goal of halving, globally, the number of starving people by 2015.

An essential task must be to at least reverse the ongoing trends toward increased atmospheric concentrations of greenhouse gases and loss of vegetation, wetlands, and small water bodies. One of the best tools for managing the heat balance of the landscape is to plant shelterbelts, which reduce wind speed and conserve water.

Apart from solar and orbital forcings, global climate conditions are created and determined mainly by three sets of factors: the physical processes and properties of the atmosphere; the chemical processes and composition of the atmosphere; and the properties of and processes at the Earth's surface. All three sets of factors are influenced by human activity, and this has been especially true during the last century (figure 1).

Andrzej Kędziora and Zbigniew W. Kundzewicz are professors at the Institute for Agricultural and Forest Environment, Polish Academy of Sciences, Poznań, Poland.

Berlin Workshop Series 2010
© 2010 The International Bank for Reconstruction and Development / The World Bank

FIGURE 1.
Factors Determining the Earth's Climatic System

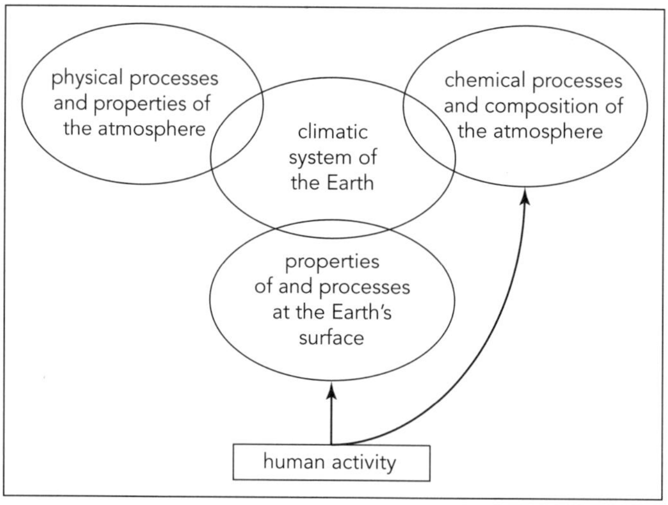

Source: Authors' elaboration.

Three processes—energy flows, cycling of matter, and global atmospheric circulation—are mainly responsible for the functioning of the climate system on different scales. The chemical and physical properties of the atmosphere (concentration of greenhouse gases, presence of aerosols and dust, and cloudiness) determine the flux of solar energy incoming in the planetary system of the Earth, as well as the sum of energy remaining in the system (greenhouse effect). But the interaction between the atmosphere and the Earth's surface influences the effect of these three processes.

The thermal conditions of the Earth's surface and the lower atmosphere are largely dependent on the partitioning of solar flux into two fluxes: latent warm ups that drives evapotranspiration of water, and sensible heat that warms up the soil and the atmosphere. In turn, this partitioning depends on the character of the surface, mainly, the richness of vegetation and water bodies. The more intensive is the surface evaporation, the less energy remains for heating air (table 1). Bare soil uses five times more energy than forests or water bodies for air heating (Ryszkowski and Kędziora 1987).

Thus, changes in the chemical composition of the atmosphere and devegetation (especially deforestation), as well as decreases in water surface caused by human activity, are very likely responsible for vital changes in climate that have occurred in the last few decades. One of the most important transformations caused by human activity was the transformation of stable ecosystems, such as forests, pastures, and water bodies, into unstable ones—for example, arable land and urban areas (figure 2). Such changes in land use unfavorably affect the water balance structure, diminishing evapotranspiration and enhancing runoff (table 2). During a dry year, about 20 percent of the precipitation is removed from the anthropogenically

TABLE 1. Components of the Heat Balance of Various Ecosystems in Wielkopolska Region, Poland, during the Growing Season (March 21–October 31)

(millions of joules per square meter)

				Ecosystem			
				Crop fields			
Component	Water	Forest	Meadow	Rapeseed	Sugar beet	Winter wheat	Bare soil
Rn	1,883	1,730	1,494	1,551	1,536	1,536	1,575
LE	1,585	1,522	1,250	1,163	1,136	1,090	866
S	120	121	215	327	339	385	651
G	179	87	29	61	61	61	47
LE/Rn	0.84	0.88	0.84	0.75	0.74	0.71	0.55
S/Rn	0.06	0.07	0.14	0.21	0.22	0.25	0.41
S/LE	0.08	0.08	0.17	0.28	0.30	0.35	0.76

Source: Ryszkowski and Kędziora 1987.

Note: Rn, net radiation; LE, latent heat of evapotranspiration; S, sensible heat; G, soil heat.

modified landscape, whereas meadows and forests retain all the available water. During a wet year, crop fields lose as much as 40 percent of precipitation, but forests lose only 20 percent. Thus, forests and meadows are the landscape elements that conserve water, while crop fields lose water unproductively.

FIGURE 2.
Transformation of Stable into Unstable Ecosystems: Three Examples

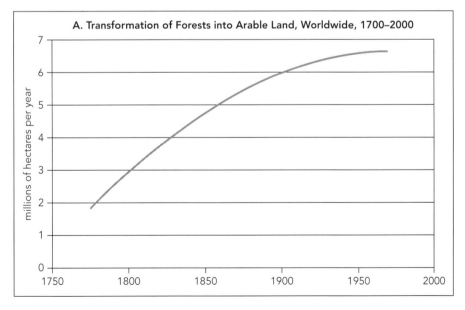

A. Transformation of Forests into Arable Land, Worldwide, 1700–2000

(continued)

FIGURE 2.
(*Continued*)

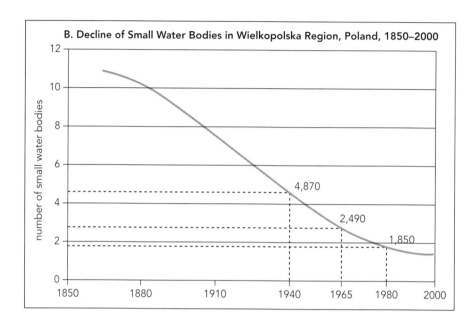

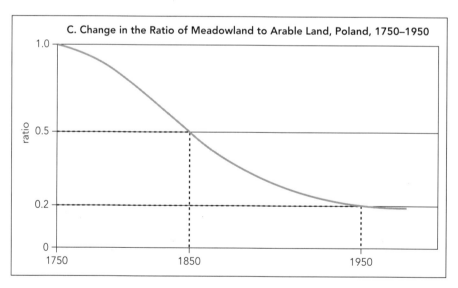

Source: Authors' elaboration.

At present, reforestation is taking place in Europe, but deforestation prevails in many countries of the Third World. Today, 40 percent of the Earth's land surface is managed for cropland and pasture, and natural forests cover another 30 percent. In developing countries, nearly 70 percent of the population lives in rural areas, where

TABLE 2. Impact of Land Use on Groundwater Discharge, Brandenburg State, Germany, Mean Values over Several Years

(millimeters per year)

Item	Dry year	Long-term average	Wet year
Annual precipitation	627	749	936
Ground water discharge			
Field	108	233	351
Meadow	0	155	271
Forest	0	149	181

Source: Werner et al. 1997.

TABLE 3. Change in the Share of Cereals in Total Agricultural Area, Poland, Selected Years, 1985–2005

Year	Percent
1985	48.1
1997	63.5
2002	73.9
2005	75.2

Source: Central Statistical Office, *Statistical Yearbook of the Republic of Poland,* various years.

agriculture is the largest supporter of livelihoods (Easterling et al. 2007). This illustrates the importance of agricultural land for the socioeconomy and the environment.

Agriculture will have to feed increasing human populations in the decades to come. Yet, since even now, many people are starving or undernourished, the United Nations Millennium Development Goal of reducing, globally, the number of starving people by half by 2015 will be difficult to achieve.

In Poland one can observe an increase in the grain crop area (table 3). Agricultural land currently makes up 60 percent of the country's total territory, and cereals alone account for 32 percent. Cereal fields are not only the dominant element in the countryside but also influence the distribution of many organisms and affect their prospects for survival and migration.

The influence of the plant cover structure on the sensible heat flux is illustrated by studies of the heat balance of a sugar beet field located in the vicinity of a field covered by the stubble left after the wheat harvest. The active surface of the intensively transpiring sugar beet field uses much more solar energy for water evapotranspiration than the stubble field does. This leads to large differences in the surface temperatures of these ecosystems. The difference between the surface temperature of the stubble and sugar beet fields was as much as 6.4°C on a sunny day (table 4), while the difference in air temperature over these fields at 2 meters above ground level was only 0.13°C. On a cloudy day, the differences were much smaller, reaching only 1.1°C on the active surface and disappearing at 2 meters above the ground. The large

TABLE 4. Meteorological Conditions and Heat Balance Structure for a Sugar Beet Field and a Stubble Field near Cessieres, France, on a Sunny Day and on a Cloudy Day, August 1998

Parameter	Sunny day		Cloudy day	
	Stubble	Sugar beets	Stubble	Sugar beets
Meteorological conditions				
Radiation temperature of active surface (°C)	26.36	19.99	15.37	14.27
Air temperature at 2 meters above ground (°C)	19.49	19.36	14.87	14.87
Wind speed at 0.5 meters above ground (meters per second, ms^{-1})	1.63	2.42	0.63	2.42
Wind speed at 2.0 meters above ground (ms^{-1})	1.97	2.92	0.76	2.92
Vertical gradient of air temperature (°C per meter, $°Cm^{-1}$)	−3.43	−0.42	−0.25	0.40
Vertical gradient of wind speed (per second, s^{-1})	0.53	1.20	0.63	1.44
Aerodynamic resistance (seconds per meter, sm^{-1})	93.0	47.0	46.0	23.0
Heat balance				
Net radiation (RN) (watts per square meter, Wm^{-2})	184.2	269.6	48.9	70.1
Sensible heat flux density (S) (Wm^{-2})	−108.3	−46.0	−10.9	18.1
Soil heat flux density (G) (Wm^{-2})	−18.4	−22.5	−5.1	−5.2
Latent heat flux density (LE) (Wm^{-2})	−57.5	−201.1	−32.9	−83.0
Bowen ratio (S/LE)	1.88	0.23	0.33	−0.22
Alpha ratio (LE/Rn)	0.31	0.75	0.67	1.18

Source: Authors' measurements.

Note: Observations were taken on August 19, 2008, a sunny day (relative sunshine, 0.746), and on August 22, 1998, a cloudy day (relative sunshine, 0.146). Daily values are averages over the period 7 a.m.–8 p.m. The sugar beets were 45 centimeters high; the stubble was 15 centimeters high.

vertical gradient of the air temperature near the surface strata indicates that on a sunny day, much of the sensible heat is transmitted from the Earth's surface to the atmosphere, enhancing air turbulence. This process intensifies the exchange of mass in the boundary layer through, for example, evapotranspiration. Such a situation is characteristic of anticyclonal circulation. In summer, in the landscape under study, such circulation occurs about 40 percent of the time.

The vertical gradient of air temperature on a sunny day was nearly nine times higher over the stubble field than over the sugar beet field. On a cloudy day, the vertical gradient over the stubble field was negative and was 14 times smaller than on a sunny day, but the vertical gradient over the sugar beet field was positive. This outcome is, of course, the result of plant transpiration, which uses more energy than the amount available from the sun. The transpiring sugar beet plants make up for the lost energy from the air, causing temperature inversion. Thus, bare soils or anthropogenically dried surfaces are the areas where convection is generated, influencing energy and mass exchange on the local scale, as well as on a regional scale. The vertical gradient of wind speed was higher over the sugar beet field than over the stubble field because of the greater roughness of the sugar beet field, which to some extent compensates for the effects described above.

The net radiation of the stubble field, 184 watts per square meter (Wm^{-2}) was much lower than the net radiation of the sugar beet field $(270\ Wm^{-2})$, mainly because of much higher reflection of solar radiation, as expressed by the albedo. This difference was much less on a cloudy day (see table 4). The active surface of the sugar beet field used nearly four times more energy on a sunny day and almost three times more on a cloudy day for evapotranspiration than did the stubble field, but the stubble field used 2.5 times more energy for air heating than did the sugar beet field on a sunny day. On a cloudy day the stubble field warmed up the air, whereas the sugar beet field cooled it.

Generally, it can be stated that biologically active ecosystems damp down the vertical exchange of sensible energy between the earth and the atmosphere and that biologically inactive ecosystems (bare soil; stubble fields) intensify these processes.

Land-Use Changes and Their Effects on Natural Resources in the Agricultural Landscape

Errors in management of the agricultural landscape, particularly during the last century, have brought about many threats in the landscape. The most important of these are an increasing water deficit, soil degradation, erosion, water pollution, and impoverishment of biodiversity.

Over decades, erroneous guidelines for melioration practices focused mainly on drainage of wet soils and reduction of small water bodies, neglecting the accumulation of water within catchments and causing a deep water deficit (figure 3). This deficit was exacerbated by soil and habitat degradation. In Poland, for example, the compaction of the soil by heavy machinery, as well as reduction of organic matter content in the soil, decreased the water capacity and water retention of the landscape. Drying of the soil, destruction of shelterbelts and shrubs, and filling of midfield ditches created conditions for sandstorms (figure 4). Farmers applied large quantities of fertilizer—usually in excess of soil capacity and more than plants could use. Nonutilized fertilizer was leached into groundwater (especially in light soil) and caused significant water pollution (figure 5). Farmers' desire for very high yields led to simplification of crop rotation and of the plant cover structure, which brought about a decline in the flora and fauna of the agricultural landscape. Monoculture may enable short-term income maximization, but it has adverse long-term effects in comparison with heterogeneous landscapes characterized by different crops, but also by islands and rows of trees and bushes (shelterbelts), strips of meadow, and so on. Natural land resources are being degraded through soil erosion, salinization of irrigated areas, dryland degradation from overgrazing, overextraction of groundwater, growing susceptibility to disease, buildup of pest resistance (favored by the spread of monocultures and the use of pesticides), loss of biodiversity, and erosion of the genetic resource base when modern varieties displace traditional ones.

FIGURE 3.
Moisture Conditions of Polish Grasslands, 1970 and 1989

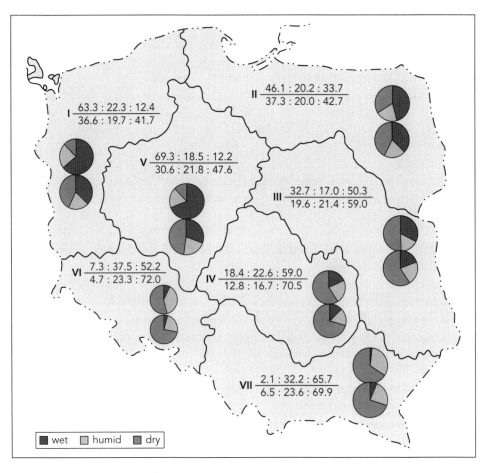

Source: Adapted from Denisiuk et al. (1992).

Note: Regions of Poland are indicated by roman numerals. The top pie graph in each region is for 1970, and the bottom one is for 1989. Numerals refer to percent of grassland in each moisture category. Categories are as follows: wet (flooded for prolonged periods), humid (periodically flooded), dry (never flooded).

The effects of land cover on microclimatic conditions (temperature, moisture, wind speed, and so on) are well known. The feedback of those modifications to mesoscale air circulation, cloud formation, and precipitation is less recognized. This information is crucial for integrating microscale modifications into global circulation models. Stohlgren et al. (1998) provide data indicating that land-use practices on the plains of Colorado in the United States influence regional climate and, in this way, indirectly affect the vegetation in adjacent areas of the Rocky Mountains.

FIGURE 4.
Sandstorm in the Vicinity of Turew, Poland

Source: Photo by Jerzy Karg.

FIGURE 5.
Change in Nitrogen Concentration in Groundwater beneath Fields (F) and Pine Forest
(P), Turew, Poland, 1993

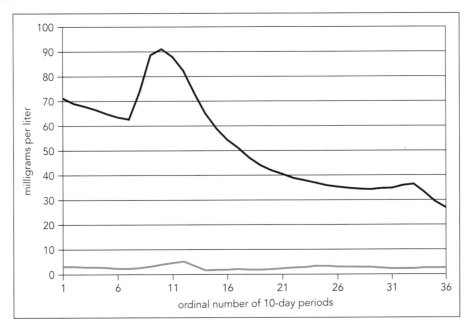

Source: Authors' elaboration.

Note: For the field, the mean concentration is 52.4 milligrams per liter; coefficient of variation (CV), 36 percent. For the pine forest, the mean concentration is 2.7 milligrams per liter; CV, 27 percent.

Climate Variability and Change and Their Effects on Natural Resources in the Agricultural Landscape

Despite climatic changes in the second millennium, such as the Medieval Optimum (800–1300) and the Little Ice Age that ended around 1850, climate was typically assumed to be nearly stable, albeit subject to high natural variability. Such climatic variables as temperature and precipitation deviated from mean values that were considered constant over a longer period. Nowadays, however, one cannot really view climate as stable and its variability as stationary. As Milly et al. (2008) put it, stationarity is dead.

An increasing body of evidence testifies to discernible ubiquitous global warming on a range of scales. As noted in the Fourth Assessment Report of the Intergovernmental Panel on Climate Change (IPCC) (2001), the temperature increase in the Northern Hemisphere over the twentieth century is likely to have been greater than for any other century in the last thousand years. Global mean surface temperature has risen by 0.65°C over the last 50 years (IPCC 2007), with disproportionately large warming in the high latitudes of the Northern Hemisphere. Fourteen of the past 15 years are among the 15 globally warmest years on record (that is, since 1850). Most of the observed increase in global mean air temperature since the mid-twentieth century is very likely attributable to the intensification of the greenhouse effect caused by the human-induced increase in concentrations of greenhouse gases in the atmosphere.

Observed and predicted climate changes will increasingly influence the processes and threats mentioned above. Rising air temperature, together with higher net radiation, will cause an increasing saturation water deficit in the atmosphere (figure 6). This will lead to a great increase in potential and real evapotranspiration, mainly in winter. As indicated by Kundzewicz et al. (2008), a shift in winter precipitation from snow to rain, and a likely increase in winter precipitation as temperatures rise, lead to increased surface runoff and reduction of soil water storage in many regions. The spring peak of snowmelt-caused runoff is advanced, or entirely eliminated, and winter flows increase. This, together with increasing winter evaporation, will reduce the possibility of replenishing soil water storage, leading to greater frequency of dry periods in summer and reduction of farmers' crop yields.

Increased frequency of extreme precipitation will also lead to water erosion of the soil. Decreased actual evapotranspiration in summer will cause reduction of latent heat flux, and so more energy remains for heating the air. The amount of energy needed to evaporate a 1 millimeter water layer can heat a layer of air 33 meters thick by 60°C. The kinetics of the atmosphere will lead to an increase in wind speed and in the frequency and intensity of storms and tornados and will consequently exacerbate wind erosion.

Increased temperature and precipitation extremes will damage plants and small animals. A lower ratio of summer to winter precipitation (figure 7) and the process of aridification have caused climate conditions in Poland to become similar to those in the Mediterranean region—a process known as mediterranization. These changes are not favorable for native flora and fauna and cause a proliferation of invasive, alien, species of plants and animals. In addition, new pests, fungi, diseases, and weeds

FIGURE 6.
Meteorological Conditions Leading to Changes in Evaporation from a Lake in
Wielkopolska Region, Poland, 1996–2006

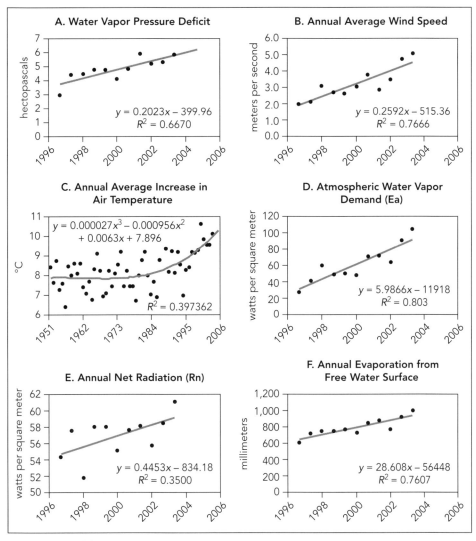

Source: Authors' elaboration.

Note: Increases in the deficit of saturation water vapor (A), in wind speed (B), and in air temperature (C) result in increased atmospheric water vapor demand (D), which, together with net radiation (E), greatly increase evaporation from the lake (F).

are expected to emerge. Altogether, this development diminishes the biodiversity of agricultural landscapes.

The distribution of the effects of climate change on agriculture will produce losers and winners. Aggregate indicators show that for a global temperature rise of 2–3°C,

FIGURE 7.
Ratio of Warm Season to Cold Season Precipitation and Total Annual Precipitation, Wielkopolska Region, Poland, 2003–07

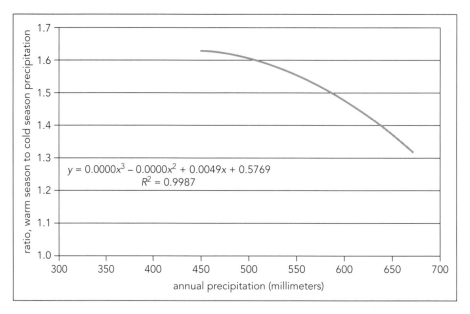

$$y = 0.0000x^3 - 0.0000x^2 + 0.0049x + 0.5769$$
$$R^2 = 0.9987$$

Source: Authors' elaboration.

Note: The warm season is April through September; the cold season is October through March.

associated with an increase in carbon dioxide (CO_2) and changes in rainfall, average productivity may increase but will then decline as warming continues. Even slight warming would worsen the situation of developing countries, with yield reductions at lower latitudes and increases in the numbers of people at risk of hunger. Globally, there should be major gains of potential agricultural land by the 2080s, particularly in North America (20–50 percent) and the Russian Federation (40–70 percent). Substantial losses (up to 9 percent) are predicted, however, for Sub-Saharan Africa because of increased drought frequency.

Agriculture in Europe is limited by temperature in the North and Northeast and by moisture in the South and Southeast. Climate change is likely to reduce the former limitation and to exacerbate the latter. It is likely, however, that in forthcoming decades the average aggregate impact of climate-related change on agriculture in Europe will be positive. Projections show a considerable increase in the area suitable for grain maize production in Europe by the end of the twenty-first century. Gains in the agricultural area and extension of the length of the growing season are expected in the North of Europe, but shrinkage of the agricultural area is likely in the South. Even a little warming and reduction in precipitation will jeopardize crop yields in southern Europe, where disadvantages are likely to predominate.

Large displacements in agricultural production are expected. Some warmer-season crops that currently grow mostly in southern Europe (for example, maize, sunflower, soybeans, grapes, and olive trees) will move northward and will become viable farther north or at higher-altitude areas in the south. Some energy crops (rape oilseed, for example), starch crops (potatoes and so on), cereals (such as barley) and solid bio-fuel crops such as sorghum and *Miscanthus* are projected to expand northward, but a reduction in southern Europe is likely. A point to be noted is that if winter rainfall rises, so will nutrient leaching—for example, in otherwise beneficially affected Scandinavia.

The projected changes in the frequency and severity of extreme climate events (for example, spells of high temperature, drought, and intense precipitation) will have significant and adverse consequences for food and forestry production and for food security. They are expected to reduce average crop yields and livestock productivity beyond the impacts attributable to changes in mean variables alone, creating the possibility of surprises. Excessive heat and lack of water during sensitive phases of plant development (for example, during the anthesis, or flowering, of wheat) drastically reduce crop yields. Abundance of water (flooding of a field, for instance) or prolonged precipitation also adversely affect crops and increase water-caused soil erosion.

Increasing climate variability will lead to greater variability in yields. It will influence the risks of fire and of pest and pathogen outbreaks, with negative consequences for food, fiber, and forestry.

Europe experienced a particularly extreme climate event during the summer of 2003, with temperatures up to 6°C above long-term means and with precipitation deficits up to 300 millimeters. Crop yields dropped by about 20 percent, and by more in much of southern Europe. The uninsured economic losses for the agriculture sector in the European Union were estimated at 13 billion euros (Easterling et al. 2007).

Rising concentrations of atmospheric carbon dioxide, lengthening of the growing season because of warming, nitrogen deposition, and changed management have resulted in a steady increase in the annual carbon dioxide storage capacity of forests and an increase in global net primary production and biomass. The overall trend toward longer growing seasons is consistent with an increase in the "greenness" of vegetation, reflecting changes in biological activity (Easterling et al. 2007). The warming, however, can also change the disturbance regime of forests by extending the range of some damaging insects (Rosenzweig et al. 2007). Rising temperatures may facilitate the dispersal of insects, enhancing their survival from one year to the next and improving conditions for new insect vectors that are now limited by colder temperatures. The existence of multiple stresses such as limited availability of water resources, loss of biodiversity, and air pollution leads to increased sensitivity to climate change and to reduction of resilience in the agriculture sector.

The reaction of forest ecosystems to climate change is a special problem. The division of the world into large biogeographic regions corresponds to climate zones: climate variables such as temperature and rainfall create natural boundaries for species distribution. Changes in current temperature, humidity, and rainfall characteristics will most certainly affect the distribution of plant species. This hypothesis is supported by paleobotanical and ecophysiologic research, extensive observation of ecosystems, and computer simulations.

The predicted changes concern the primary forest-creating species, which may lose their current optimum habitat and will be subject to all the consequences of this fact, in the form of biochemical and physiological changes that will occur first in phenol-ogy and then in productivity and that will affect plant health, susceptibility to known and unknown biotic threats, and resilience to factors of the abiotic environment. It is hard to predict all the possible consequences for the forest economy and the health status of forests, as the changes will not be limited to the species level but will spread to the ecosystem and landscape levels.

The potential reactions of forest ecosystems to climate change may be classified as follows:

- Changes in forest location
- Changes in forest structure
- Changes in forest productivity.

Climate changes and the movement of climate zones may be faster than changes in locations of plant communities, and this may lead to changes in forest areas and in carbon sequestration potential (Smith and Shugart 1993). This is of crucial impor-tance for the location of natural forests. It is a lesser problem for managed forests and plantations, where foresters are able to plant seeds according to the climatic prefer-ences of species, assuming that past recognition of those preferences is still up to date (Davis and Shaw 2001).

An especially important, complicated, and most uncertain issue is that of the impact of increased carbon dioxide levels on forest productivity. Many opinions sug-gest at least a temporary increase in biomass growth if a "fertilizing effect" occurs. The effect of "carbon fertilizing" on an ecosystem level will be limited by competi-tion, insufficient levels of other nutrition elements such as water and minerals, and disturbances (insects, disease, fires, wind, and so on).

Forests, representing an intensively evaporative ecosystem, are very important in shaping the water cycle and the structure of the water balance (Pielke et al. 1998; Pielke 2001). Under convective conditions, water evaporated from the forest returns partly into local or regional cycling, increasing the amount of precipitation. It is esti-mated that a 1 percent rise in the percentage of forest may increase annual precipi-tation by 5 millimeters (Bac 1968). This increase is higher in the warm period than in winter because of a greater probability of convective conditions in the summer. For Poland, the optimal share of forests in the landscape area is 35 percent; currently, it is 29 percent, but reforestation is going on.

Interaction between Climate and Land Use

Climate change and its impacts are closely interlinked with land surface processes dependent on land use and land cover. The role of land surface in climate variability and change is often underestimated. However, the thermal conditions of the Earth's surface and the lower atmosphere largely depend on the structure of the Earth's sur-face energy budget. In particular, partitioning of the incoming solar flux into latent heat (driving evapotranspiration) and sensible heat, which is responsible for heating the soil and atmosphere, plays an important role. This partitioning is driven by the structure of the land surface, in particular, by vegetation cover and inland water bodies. The more intensive is evaporation, the less energy remains for air heating. Changes in the composition of the atmosphere and the properties of the land surface are responsible for most of the climate change during the past decades.

Over bare land, the sensible heat flux dominates over the latent heat flux, resulting in heating of the air and the soil via the "oven" effect. Over a forest, the substantial latent heat flux does not allow heating of the air and the soil.

Changes in water availability are the integrated result of natural factors (such as volume and timing of precipitation, catchment storage, evapotranspiration, snowmelt, and whether precipitation falls as snow or rain), as well as of watershed management practices and river engineering that alter the water conveyance system over time. It is difficult to disentangle the climatic effects from the effects of such human interventions in the catchment as reservoir construction and changes in land use and land cover (e.g., deforestation or afforestation, urbanization, and agricultural activities). This latter group of factors also affects climatic variables via the albedo and the heat and water balance. Changes in precipitation, temperature, energy availability, atmospheric humidity, and wind speed, as well as the plant physiology effects of increased atmospheric carbon dioxide concentration, influence evapotranspiration and runoff.

Management Aspects

Since warming is going on and will accelerate, adaptation is a must. What can be done? Agriculture can adapt to climate change through short-term adjustments such as changes in agronomic practices (date of planting, harvesting, external inputs, fertilizers, and so on) and long-term changes (land use; development of suitable crop types adapted to the changing conditions in the location and resistant to water, weeds, and pests). Since irrigation demand is likely to grow while water availability drops, improvements in the efficiency of irrigation are needed. Options for adapting to drier conditions include introduction of new drought-resistant varieties, intercropping, crop residue retention, conservative tillage, weed management, and water harvesting (Easterling et al. 2007). Improved efficiency of water use in irrigation ("more crops per drop"), increased resistance to heat shock and drought, and more effective use of water in areas with declines in rainfall are particularly important because globally, in volumetric terms, irrigated agriculture is the main water user.

Phenological changes are often followed by changes in farmers' management practices, such as altering the timing or location of cropping activities (e.g., advancing seeding and sowing dates). Among other measures are changes in agrotechnical practices to conserve soil moisture—for example, through retention of crop residues and the use of crop rotation; the introduction of new cultivars (e.g., selection of varieties or species with more appropriate thermal time and vernalization requirements);

modification of fertilizer rates to maintain grain or fruit quality consistent with the climate; and adjustment of the amounts and timing of irrigation and other water management practices (using drought-tolerant crops, with higher drought resistance and longer grain filling). Soil should be protected against erosion (from surface runoff, flash floods, and the like) and against negative effects caused by cultivation. Appropriate measures include reduction of use of organic fertilizers and changes in the structure of agricultural crops. Soil moisture should be conserved by, for example, mulching. Extension of irrigated agriculture may not be feasible everywhere. For instance, Polish agriculture is mostly rainfed, and, as a result of scanty and variable precipitation and the dominating lowland character of the country—meaning a scarcity of sites for water storage reservoirs—available water volumes will not be sufficient for massive agricultural irrigation.

The various options for adapting to the impacts of climate change on agriculture carry different costs—from changing practices in place, to changing locations. The effectiveness of adaptation ranges from marginally reducing negative impacts to changing a negative impact into a positive one. On average, in cereal-cropping systems worldwide, adaptations such as altering varieties and planting times enable avoidance of a 10–15 percent reduction in yield for a 1–2°C local temperature increase. Adaptation, however, imposes stresses on water and environmental resources as warming increases. Adaptive capacity in low latitudes is estimated to be exceeded at a 3°C local temperature increase (Easterling et al. 2007).

As yields drop, pressures to cultivate marginal land or adopt unsustainable cultivation practices may increase land degradation and resource use and endanger biodiversity. A feasible long-term adaptation measure is to adjust the allocation of agricultural land according to its changing suitability under climate change. Large-scale abandonment of cropland in Europe may provide an opportunity to increase the cultivation of bioenergy crops. Different types of agricultural adaptation (intensification, extensification, and abandonment) may be appropriate (Alcamo et al. 2007).

Investigations show that landscape structure is the most important factor determining the natural resistance of the environment to threats. The more mosaic-like is the structure of the landscape, the higher is the degree of the landscape's resistance and resilience to disturbances such as disease. The landscape structure can be improved through introduction of forests, shelterbelts, meadow strips, and bushes; restoration of damaged postglacial ponds; and maintenance of wetlands and riparian ecosystems. Enhancement of ecotones and biogeochemical barriers is the most efficient tool for controlling energy flow and matter cycling in the landscape—processes that are necessary for sustainable agriculture (figure 8).

Increases in wetland and forest areas can, to some degree, offset increasing carbon dioxide concentration in the atmosphere. Wetlands in temperate zones can sequester about 2 tons of carbon per hectare per year. Forest ecosystems can sequester carbon in the tree biomass and about 0.3 tons per hectare per year in the soil. But it has to be kept in mind that forests absorb carbon only during periods of growth; mature forest does not sequester carbon. Carbon can also be sequestered by arable land. If good agricultural practices are employed, the increased organic matter in the 30-centimeter-deep plowed layer of soil can reach about 1 ton per hectare per year.

FIGURE 8.
Influence of Plant Cover Structure on Nitrogen Concentration in Water Output from Drainage Basin in Growing Season (March 21–October 31), Turew, Wielkopolska Region, Poland

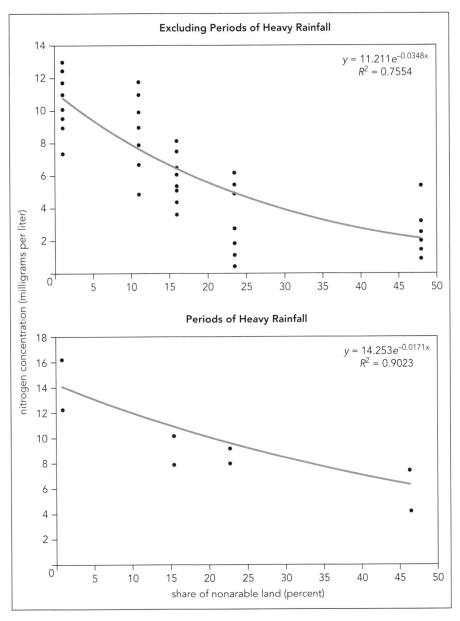

Excluding Periods of Heavy Rainfall

$y = 11.211e^{-0.0348x}$
$R^2 = 0.7554$

Periods of Heavy Rainfall

$y = 14.253e^{-0.0171x}$
$R^2 = 0.9023$

nitrogen concentration (milligrams per liter)

share of nonarable land (percent)

Source: Authors' elaboration.

Carbon storage in global plant cover amounts to 466 gigatons, whereas carbon storage in global soils (to the depth of 1 meter) is estimated as 2,011 gigatons.

Shelterbelts introduced into grain monoculture landscapes change the microclimatic conditions of the field, as well as the aerodynamic characteristics of an active surface. By reducing wind speed and stomatal resistance and increasing humidity, turbulence, and net radiation, shelterbelts cause a slight increase in the actual evapotranspiration of the landscape taken as a whole, but evapotranspiration decreases in the cultivated fields lying between shelterbelts.

The number of biogeochemical barriers in a landscape rises along with the increased complexity of the landscape. The nutrient content in groundwater is greatly reduced when water flows under shelterbelts or meadow strips. A shelterbelt or meadow strip a dozen or so meters wide reduces nitrate concentration by 50 to 90 percent and diminishes phosphorus concentration by 90 percent or more. The amount of nitrates leached from a uniform arable catchment is many times higher than from a mosaic watershed.

The content of soil organic matter is one of the most important factors determining the water storage capacity and other properties of the soil. Organic matter can absorb 10 times more water than can mineral soils. In addition, organic matter improves the structure of the soil and increases the amount of macro- and mesopores, which improve water availability for plants. In brief, increased organic matter content in the soil improves soil fertility.

Control of the structure of the agricultural landscape is important for mitigation of climate change and adaptation to climate change and its impacts. Through use of shelterbelts, carbon can be sequestered from atmospheric carbon dioxide and stored in plant tissue and in the soil. Shelterbelts introduced into a cereal monoculture landscape change the microclimate of the field, as well as the aerodynamic characteristics of the active surface. Auxiliary benefits of a shelterbelt include provision of shelter for fauna, creation of ecological corridors enhancing migration (with benefits for biodiversity), greater water quantity (longer snow cover), better water quality (extraction of nutrients from groundwater), soil conservation, windbreaks, provision of forest products (wood, mushrooms, berries, and so on), and aesthetics. Shelterbelts counteract adverse effects related to water balance changes, remediate water pollution, and enhance biodiversity. Thus, they contribute to conservation of all three natural resources—water, soil, and biodiversity.

Final Remarks

In order to counteract undesirable climatic tendencies, people must reverse the trends toward increased atmospheric concentrations of greenhouse gases and loss of vegetation, wetlands, and small water bodies. Certainly, reduction of greenhouse gas concentrations and restoration of vegetation, wetlands, and water bodies are much needed.

Introduction of shelterbelts into a simplified landscape is one of the best tools for managing the heat balance of the landscape. Shelterbelts reduce wind speed and conserve the water supply of fields located between shelterbelts, but they increase sensible heat flux somewhat (table 5). In periods of strong advection of dry and warm air, irrigated fields can conserve 10 percent of water during evapotranspiration, in comparison with a landscape without shelterbelts.

TABLE 5. Impact of Landscape Structure on the Heat and Water Balance during the Growing Season (March 21–October 31), Vicinity of Turew, Poland

Landscape type	Rn (Wm^{-2})	LE (Wm^{-2})	S (Wm^{-2})	ETP (mm)	ETR (mm)	ETR/ETP	ETR/OP
Grain crop monoculture	1,542	1,035	495	650	414	0.64	1.10
Grain crops with shelterbelts	1,586	1,078	496	586	431	0.76	1.15
Grain crops with windbreaks	1,567	1,010	546	581	404	0.86	1.08
Grain crops without shelterbelts, under convection	1,586	1,258	315	898	503	0.56	1.34
Grain crops with shelterbelts, under advection	1,586	1,181	412	592	464	0.78	1.24

Source: Authors' measurements.

Note: RN, net radiation; LE, latent heat of evapotranspiration; S, sensible heat; ETP, potential evapotranspiration; ETR, real evapotranspiration; OP, precipitation; Wm^{-2}, watts per square meter; mm, millimeters.

References

Alcamo, Joseph, José M. Moreno, Belá Nováky, Marco Bindi, Roman Corobov, R. J. N. Devoy, Christos Giannakopoulos, Eric Martin, Jørgen E. Olesen, and Anatoly Shvidenko. 2007. "Europe." In *Climate Change 2007: Impacts, Adaptation and Vulnerability. Contribution of Working Group II to the Fourth Assessment Report of the Intergovernmental Panel on Climate Change*, ed. Martin L. Parry, Osvaldo F. Canziani, Jean P. Palutikof, Paul J. van der Linden, and Claire E. Hanson, 541–80. Cambridge, U.K.: Cambridge University Press.

Bac, S. 1968. The role of forest in water balance. [in Polish.] *Folia Forestalia Polonica* Series A, 14: 5–65.

Central Statistical Office. Various years. *Statistical Yearbook of the Republic of Poland.* Warsaw: Central Statistical Office of Poland.

Davis, Margaret B., and Ruth G. Shaw. 2001. "Range Shift and Adaptive Responses to Quaternary Climate Change." *Science* 292 (April 27): 673–79.

Denisiuk, Z., A. Kalemba, T. Zając, A. Ostrowska, S. Gawliński, J. Sienkiewicz, and M. Rejman-Czajkowska. 1992. *Integration between Agriculture and Nature Conservation in Poland.* International Union for Conservation of Nature (IUCN) East European Programme. Gland, Switzerland: IUCN.

Easterling, William E., Pramod K. Aggarwal, Punsalmaa Batima, Keith M. Brander, Lin Erda, S. Mark Howden, Andrei Kirilenko, John Morton, Jean-François Soussana, Josef Schmidhuber, and Francesco N. Tubiello. 2007. "Food, Fibre and Forest Products." In *Climate Change 2007: Impacts, Adaptation and Vulnerability. Contribution of Working Group II to the Fourth Assessment Report of the Intergovernmental Panel on Climate Change*, ed. Martin L. Parry, Osvaldo F. Canziani, Jean P. Palutikof, Paul J. van der Linden, and Claire E. Hanson, 273–313. Cambridge, U.K.: Cambridge University Press.

IPCC (Intergovernmental Panel on Climate Change). 2001. "Summary for Policymakers." In *Climate Change 2001: The Physical Science Basis. Contribution of Working Group I to the Fourth Assessment Report of the Intergovernmental Panel on Climate Change.* Cambridge, U.K.: Cambridge University Press.

————. 2007. "Summary for Policymakers." In *Climate Change 2007: The Physical Science Basis. Contribution of Working Group I to the Fourth Assessment Report of the Intergovernmental Panel on Climate Change.* Cambridge, U.K.: Cambridge University Press. http://www1.ipcc.ch/pdf/assessment-report/ar4/wg1/ar4-wg1-spm.pdf.

Kundzewicz, Z. W., L. J. Mata, N. Arnell, P. Döll, B. Jiménez, K. Miller, T. Oki, Z. Şen, and I. Shiklomanov. 2008. "The Implications of Projected Climate Change for Freshwater Resources and Their Management." *Hydrological Sciences Journal* 53 (1): 3–10.

Milly, P. C. D., Julio Betancourt, Malin Falkenmark, Robert M. Hirsch, Zbigniew W. Kundzewicz, Dennis P. Lettenmaier, and Ronald J. Stouffer. 2008. "Stationarity Is Dead: Whither Water Management?" *Science* 319 (February 1): 573–74.

Pielke, Roger A., Sr. 2001. "Influence of the Spatial Distribution of Vegetation and Soils on the Prediction on Cumulus Convective Rainfall." *Reviews of Geophysics* 39 (2): 151–77.

Pielke, Roger A., Sr., Roni Avissar, Michael Raupach, A. Johannes Dolman, Xubin Zeng, and A. Scott Denning. 1998. "Interactions between the Atmosphere and Terrestrial Ecosystems: Influence on Weather and Climate." *Global Change Biology* 4 (5, June): 461–75.

Rosenzweig, Cynthia, Gino Casassa, David J. Karoly, Anton Imeson, Chunzhen Liu, Annette Menzel, Samuel Rawlins, Terry L. Root, Bernard Seguin, and Piotr Tryjanowski. 2007. "Assessment of Observed Changes and Responses in Natural and Managed Systems." In *Climate Change 2007: Impacts, Adaptation and Vulnerability. Contribution of Working Group II to the Fourth Assessment Report of the Intergovernmental Panel on Climate Change,* ed. Martin L. Parry, Osvaldo F. Canziani, Jean P. Palutikof, Paul J. van der Linden, and Claire E. Hanson, 79–131. Cambridge, U.K.: Cambridge University Press.

Ryszkowski, L., and A. Kędziora. 1987. "Impact of Agricultural Landscape Structure on Energy Flow and Water Cycling." *Landscape Ecology* 1 (2): 85–94.

————. 1995. "Modification of the Effects of Global Climate Change by Plant Cover Structure in an Agricultural Landscape." *Geographia Polonica* 65: 5–34.

Smith, T. M., and H. H. Shugart. 1993. "The Transient Response of Terrestrial Carbon Storage to a Perturbed Climate." *Nature* 361 (February 11): 523–26.

Stohlgren, Thomas J., Thomas N. Chase, Roger A. Pielke, Sr., Timothy G. F. Kittel, and Jill S. Baron. 1998. "Evidence That Local Land Use Practices Influence Regional Climate, Vegetation and Stream Flow Patterns in Adjacent Natural Areas." *Global Change Biology* 4 (5, June): 495–504.

Werner, A., F. Eulenstein, U. Schindler, L. Müller, L. Ryszkowski, and A. Kędziora. 1997. "Grundwasserneubildung und Landnutzung." *Zeitschrift für Kulturtechnik und Landentwicklung* 38: 106–13.

Part IV
Development, Non-State Actors, and Climate Governance: Private Sector and NGOs

Climate Change and the Threat to Development

DAVID ROGERS

The threat to sustainable development caused by climate change and natural hazards is significant and is growing. Countries are wrestling with the need to mitigate climate impacts in the long term, but adaptation offers the only way of coping with the inevitable effects of climate change over the next few decades. Developing economies are particularly vulnerable; not only are they predominantly poor and exposed to natural hazards, but many lack the capacity to provide climate risk information to their own citizens or to manage disaster risk effectively. Few of these countries possess dedicated climate services. This paper describes the emerging role of national meteorological and hydrological services (NMHSs) in developing countries and examines some issues surrounding their activities.

Mainstreaming the reduction of climate change risks into development is a priority that requires the translation of existing international commitments into action. Support by the international community for construction of national monitoring and dissemination programs must be accompanied by institution building aimed at enabling governments to incorporate climate information into economic development programs. Collaboration by a wide range of stakeholders is needed to promote understanding of and response to the implications of climate change for disaster risk and development.

Climate change threatens to reduce or even reverse the gains made toward sustainable development. The threat is complex because it comes not only from the environment itself but also from climate change policy decisions. Addressing the latter requires that climate change be integrated into the existing social and economic processes that are currently driving development. A holistic approach will require the

David Rogers is president of the Health and Climate Foundation, Washington, DC.

Berlin Workshop Series 2010

© 2010 The International Bank for Reconstruction and Development / The World Bank

integration of social, economic, and environmental information to permit a full understanding of the impact of climate on development and to inform policy decisions in all the interconnected sectors—health, energy, agriculture, urban development, and so on.

In general, climate change has a multiplicative effect on existing problems. For example, water stress will likely worsen in places already suffering from drought; disease epidemics will increase; and so on. The impacts of the choices made to mitigate climate change are less clear because of the interconnections between various social and economic sectors. Recent experience with certain kinds of biofuels is one example of how what appears to be a renewable replacement for a nonrenewable, carbon-based energy source can distort the commodity market and increase food insecurity for millions of people.

The Stern Review, carried out for the U.K. government, highlights the severity of the climate change issue and the need for immediate action to avoid an environmentally triggered massive and sustained downturn in global economies (Stern 2007). Countries are wrestling with the need to mitigate climate impacts in the long term, but adaptation offers the only way of coping with the inevitable effects of climate change over the next few decades. The capability of a country to adapt depends on its ability to monitor climate, to provide reliable scientific information and predictions of climate change, and to use this information in risk reduction actions that promote sustainable development (Rogers 2007). Developing economies are particularly vulnerable because they are predominantly poor, not very resilient, and more exposed to natural hazards, but also because many lack the capacity to provide climate risk information to their own citizens or to manage disaster risk effectively. The fact that few countries possess dedicated climate services creates opportunities for many different entities to fill the gap, with the potential for producing confusing and contradictory information that leads to ill-informed policy decisions (Rogers et al. 2008).

Mainstreaming the reduction of climate change risks into development is a priority that requires the translation of existing international commitments into action. Stern (2007) argues that the international community should support global, regional, and national research and information systems on risk and should assist developing-country governments in building adequate monitoring and dissemination programs at the national level. This effort must be accompanied by institution building aimed at developing national capability to transform climate data so that governments can incorporate climate information into economic development programs. Collaboration by a wide range of stakeholders is needed to strengthen coordination between government ministries and between government, nongovernmental organizations (NGOs), the private sector, and academia so as to promote understanding of and response to the implications of climate change for disaster risk and development.

The following sections discuss the development implications of climate change, risk management, and issues surrounding national weather services and the provision of weather-related information to the public.

Development, Climate Change, and Natural Hazards

The potential for environmental hazards and climate change to undermine development is great and is increasing (DFID 2006). Intense floods, droughts, storms, and epidemics are already having significant effects on the economic performance of developing countries and on the lives and livelihoods of millions of poor people around the world (GEF 2006; WHO 2008b). In Africa poverty reduction and national development are held back by climatic variability and extremes (GCOS 2006). It is doubtful that the United Nations Millennium Development Goals (MDGs) will be achieved in the region unless African countries become far better equipped to manage the impacts of natural disasters and climate change and unless climate and disaster risk management are included within development planning (United Nations 2000; UNDP 2004; DFID 2006; GEF 2006; Stern 2007).

In particular, climate change and weather extremes put at risk investments in infrastructure, agriculture, human health, water resources, disaster management, and the environment. For example, Africa's transportation infrastructure is crucial for lifting the region out of poverty, but every year large parts of this network are affected by flooding. The Mozambique floods of 2000 inflicted more than US$32 million of damage on the country's roads and US$7 million on its railways (DFID 2006). Climate change and weather extremes also increase the vulnerability of people—particularly the poorest—when development needs trigger investment and human settlement in coastal zones, flood plains, arid areas, and other high-risk environments. Worldwide, between 1980 and 2000 more than 1.2 million people lost their lives as a result of floods, droughts, and storms (UNDP 2004), with a total financial cost exceeding US$900 billion (Munich Re 2002).

In recent years, thanks largely to advances in forecasting and assessment, people are better prepared, and the number killed directly by extreme events has decreased. This trend, however, is unlikely to persist because developing countries continue to be exposed to frequent and extreme weather events. In addition, climate-sensitive diseases claim more than 1 million lives each year—mostly children under age 5 in developing countries—and without proper consideration of and response to the impact of climate change on human development, more people will be at risk. Climate change can trigger food insecurity: today, 20 million people in Africa rely on relief to meet their basic food needs, and in the absence of climate risk reduction strategies, the numbers will increase dramatically. The financial consequences of natural hazards and climate change for human well-being are difficult to estimate from current data, but clearly, they are large. Unless we are able to understand and reduce the vulnerability of people to climate change and natural hazards, human development itself is at risk. The U.K. Department for International Development (DFID), the second-largest bilateral humanitarian aid donor after the U.S. government, estimates that 15 percent of its development budget is spent on disaster assistance (DFID 2006). Increasing the resilience of the poor could free hundreds of millions of dollars annually for investment in sustainable development projects.

Climate change adds a new and largely uncertain dimension to the development problem by compounding the risks of natural hazards. This is evident already in many parts of the world; for example, it is estimated that 50 to 65 percent of development assistance in Nepal is directed toward activities potentially affected by climate risks (Agrawala et al. 2005). Despite the continuing debate about the relationship between the intensity and frequency of tropical cyclones and climate change, it is clear that glacial retreat is increasing the threat of flooding and that sea-level rise is increasing the risk of coastal inundation by storm surges.

Ecosystem changes resulting from altered patterns of rainfall and temperature are changing the behavior of crop pests, human exposure to climate-sensitive diseases, the length of the growing season, and irrigation requirements. Economic losses are rising, especially in high human development countries such as those of Western Europe. Elsewhere, although the losses may be less in absolute terms, the financial impact on countries with low gross domestic product (GDP) is sufficient to halt or slow human development. The cost of the 1999–2000 droughts in Kenya, for example, represented at least 16 percent of the country's GDP (Mogaka et al. 2004).

Managing Risk

Development goals must interact with disaster risk and with climate change risk. Unless climate risks are factored into current development activities, future adaptation may be irreversibly constrained. The relationships between sustainable development, hydrometeorological hazards, and the factors that trigger human disasters are well understood (IFRC 2002; WMO 2005; DFID 2006), but much less attention has been paid to mainstreaming climate change risk into development activities (GEF 2006).

Climate change risk and disaster risk are intimately linked. Natural disaster preparedness and management not only save lives but can also promote early and cost-effective adaptation to climate risks (Stern 2007). Many studies have estimated that the internal rate of return from disaster reduction initiatives is between 20 and 50 percent and that these initiatives often provide additional, sometimes unanticipated, social benefits. For example, flood alleviation projects both increase the availability of water for irrigation and offset the impacts of drought.

A recent analysis of national development plans, poverty reduction strategy papers, sectoral strategies, and project documents in climate-sensitive sectors indicates that little or no attention is being paid to climate change and that even when it is mentioned, specific operational guidance on how to take it into account is generally lacking (Smith et al. 2005). In part, this is because the need for climate information to serve current development requirements has been lost in the discussion about policies for dealing with uncertain, scenario-based future impacts of climate change. For example, in Africa the national adaptation programs of action drawn up by ministries of the environment have had problems with engaging decision makers from other ministries who have not recognized that addressing the management of climate variability today is an essential step toward a strategy for managing climate change in the future (GCOS 2006). A lack of institutional coordination for facilitating systematic integration of climate information into the planning process is another major problem (Rogers et al. 2008).

The World Bank has identified climate change as a risk management issue for development and has begun to factor this risk into its development project cycle, with the dual purpose of protecting its investments and improving the impact of development efforts (GEF 2006). Critical steps are the mainstreaming of climate risk management into countries' economic planning and the building of capacity in ministries of finance and economic planning for using climate information to manage risks to public sector investments (Bettencourt et al. 2006). For example, in a long-term program to help Kiribati adapt to climate change, a Global Environment Facility (GEF) project was started in the Ministry of Finance and Economic Planning and was then moved to a National Strategic Risk Management Unit in the Office of the President, highlighting the importance of the effort for Kiribati's development strategy (GEF 2006).

In the private sector, insurance markets have emerged as a means of managing disaster and climate risk where the probability of occurrence is relatively low. They create incentives for participants to reduce risks, and they have the added benefit of accelerating adaptation. For these markets to work effectively, however, insurance companies must have access to accurate weather and climate forecasts and impact data. Lack of access is currently a major constraint in developing countries, and it continues to limit the role of insurance in disaster risk management in the poorest parts of the world.

Climate Change Policies and the Threat to Development

It is also important to understand the potential risks for human development of specific climate change policies. It is no coincidence that the poor have the poorest health. This is a consequence of substandard living and working conditions, lack of access to fresh water and sanitation, food insecurity, and the absence of policies for addressing these inequities (WHO 2008a). It is generally believed that climate change will have a multiplicative effect on the burden of disease. Thus, the poor are likely to shoulder a disproportionate share of the consequences of climate change because of their exposure to disease and because of living conditions that will be directly threatened by an increase in the severity of natural disasters. They will also be more exposed to food and water insecurity associated with climate change.

The effect on human development and well-being of specific climate change mitigation and adaptation policies in every sector therefore needs to be carefully assessed. A cautionary example is the effort to promote biofuels in developed economies, which could have negative effects on food security and malnutrition in developing and least developed countries. To give another illustration, sustainable energy and transport policies may have potentially positive health effects in Europe, Japan, and

North America, but with little or no benefit for many people within developing countries if those policies increase energy and transport costs, forcing the poorest to seek cheaper, more polluting alternatives.

It is also important to consider the impact of investments in climate change mitigation and adaptation and to avoid redirecting resources away from existing projects focused on improving the social determinants of human health and well-being. Understanding of the impacts of climate change and climate change policy across all sectors that affect the health and well-being of societies depends on a comprehensive understanding of the impact of climate and, hence, on a comprehensive and specific system of climate observations linked to social and economic determinants applicable to development.

Role of Meteorological and Hydrological Services

The primary roles of national meteorological and hydrological services (NMHSs) in economic development are to support good practice in disaster risk reduction through risk identification, monitoring, early warning, and public awareness; to assist technical and physical risk mitigation; and to help build resilience and promote innovation, knowledge, and education (DFID 2006). These services include early warning systems for famine, drought, heat waves, hurricanes, and floods; provision of climate data to support effective water management, agricultural planning, and health care and of the information needed to assess the likely impacts of climate change; and support for climate change adaptation strategies.

Climate service providers at the national level must become part of the sustainable infrastructure, which is needed to establish strong coordination mechanisms across government, to link communities and national policy makers, and to improve environmental management (Rogers et al. 2008). A national community of practice is one means of spanning all the relevant disciplines and decision-making processes so as to create a forum for shared responsibility for development. This approach explicitly recognizes that government-funded public services, such as NMHSs, and their partners have a role in assessing development risks. It is also a mechanism for encouraging partnership between the private and public sectors. One example is the initiative, which was started by the Global Humanitarian Forum and its public and private sector partners to help NMHSs improve their observing networks and service delivery.

Meteorological, climatological, and hydrological communities at all levels, from the local to the global, need to be engaged to work within the risk management and policy sectors in a way that influences both policy and practice to meet development needs (GCOS 2006). A core responsibility of government will be to see that it has access to, and disseminates domestically, good information on climate change. This information will range from forecasts of the likely timing, extent, and effects of climate change to knowledge of drought- and flood-resistant crops, new crop-planting techniques, emerging health risks, and risks to other societal and economic sectors.

Although advances have already been made in creating indicators and indexes on disaster risk, the value of these instruments lies in the ongoing availability of social, economic, and environmental vulnerability data that include climate change risks. Tools that properly assess societal risk must take into account its dynamic nature, including climate change and variability, natural hazards, urbanization, population change, the spread of disease, and political and economic changes. A goal is for decision makers to have available robust national and local risk indicators that can help decide national development policy and planning.

The current weakness in the availability of relevant climate information in many developing countries must be addressed if climate change risks are to be factored into risk reduction strategies. Central to climate risk management services is real-time environmental monitoring, without which it is difficult to produce meaningful regional and local climate change assessments. Many NMHSs in developing countries do not have the capacity to provide their governments with the necessary information. Obtaining the needed information is beyond the current capacity of many developing-country governments.

This low starting point highlights the size of the challenge. By contrast, in developed countries government-funded research programs are already in place to inform national policies (Stern 2007). Developing countries need international assistance to build adequate monitoring and dissemination programs at the national level (GCOS 2006) and to create and sustain the basic infrastructure and human resources needed to support these activities.

Both the observing networks and the NMHSs that are responsible for these networks have been neglected in many developing countries and can no longer provide even basic climate information (Washington, Harrison, and Conway 2004). Developing countries also need help to encourage collaboration between stakeholders, across government departments, and between governments, NGOs, the private sector, and academia. Partnerships are essential for transferring capacity and know-how from developed-country programs to developing countries and for providing the latter with access to global public goods.

The observing networks must span local and community needs and fulfill national and regional requirements. Their existence depends on partnerships between scientific disciplines and between different communities, with an emphasis on delivering reliable, quality-controlled, and cost-effective data that meet specific user needs in the development community. Their sustainability rests on community interest and ability to maintain them at the local level (IRI 2006). The obligation on the part of the donor community and beneficiary governments is to recognize that climate risk reduction is intrinsically tied to the ability to observe and predict changes in the environment. Therefore, any development strategy must consider the need for climate-observing networks to support development investment decisions.

Governments should make climate data available, given the public good nature of the information and its wide application for the well-being of society. Fulfillment of this task will require many developing countries to change policies that currently restrict the availability of weather and climate data. Users note frequent difficulties in obtaining weather, climate, and water information, with obvious adverse consequences for a variety of applications, including health, agriculture, and development. The reasons for these difficulties include policies against the free dissemination of data, inadequate resources of the NMHSs that should supply the data, and a nonservice culture in which data restrictions are perceived as a means of enhancing commercial value (IRI 2006). A mechanism is needed to distinguish public sector (individual and humanitarian) users from commercial users. One possible approach is to issue a free license for unrestricted public use of data and a commercial paying license for other users. This is a particularly sensitive issue in some African countries, where data distributed through existing international agreements finds its way back to a country through commercial services that are in competition with the national meteorological service.

Even with complete, free, and open exchange of national climate data, developing countries need help with accessing the information that is available to the international community, particularly information from countries with highly developed climate change programs. The challenge for developed countries' climate services is to increase the availability of global public goods that can be used by developing countries to enhance their autonomy in creating and implementing effective climate risk reduction strategies. This approach is exemplified by the portable version of the U.K. Met Office Hadley Centre's Regional Climate Model, which is freely available to researchers in developing countries for use on standard computers. Other examples are the assessment tools that can be adapted from activities such as the U.K. Climate Impacts Programme (UKCIP).[1]

Observing Networks and the Role of Public-Private Partnerships

A long-standing priority is to improve climate-observing networks in developing countries and to increase NMHSs' capacity and capability to help their governments reduce disaster and climate change risks to development. The Global Climate Observing System Plan of Action for Africa (GCOS 2006), which addresses the specific requirements and costs of improving climate observations in that region, is already under way. To succeed, this initiative has to be accompanied by a corresponding improvement in institutional infrastructure and human resources to sustain these observing networks and to provide the scientific expertise needed by economic planners and other government departments for addressing adaptation issues.

Success in this endeavor is unlikely unless the role of the private sector as a partner of public institutions is rethought. The revolution in telecommunications throughout the world is an important development. The growth of mobile communications in many developing countries provides an opportunity to restore and expand in situ observing networks through a partnership between mobile phone companies, NMHSs, and donors. This approach is exemplified by the "Weather Info for All" project supported in part by the African Development Bank, which engages

NMHSs in a public-private initiative aimed at filling the information gap by providing basic meteorological information for African countries through the installation of weather stations throughout the continent.

These initiatives require new partnerships or consortia at the national level to ensure the widest possible use of the data and a sense of ownership of information that is essential to the success of many aspects of a country's development agenda, ranging from climate-informed central planning to the use of the data as part of a malaria control program or a food security initiative at the village level. Such community involvement demands much effort from all stakeholders to enable them to cooperate and collaborate effectively.

Several existing and nascent national initiatives may provide some direction here. In particular, the recent growth in partnerships between NMHSs and ministries of health has led to new kinds of consortia involving government departments and other civil society stakeholders. This has been implemented and documented in Ethiopia (see, e.g., Ghebreyesus et al. 2008) and is in development in Madagascar, Kenya, and West African countries. It should be relatively easy to expand these initiatives and to establish similar national consortia wherever they are needed. A key element is the sense of co-ownership between the providers and users of climate information.

Education and Training

NMHSs need to put greater emphasis on training so that they can move beyond forecasting toward synthesis and adaptation of weather, climate, and water information to meet the needs of their countries' societal and economic decision makers. For example, the Commission for Climatology of the World Meteorological Organization (WMO) has developed expert teams to increase capability in urban and building climatology, human health, and energy, among other fields.[2] Although NMHSs will continue to provide weather-related information for day-to-day decision making, they must become more involved in assessments and longer-term societal planning. This institutional change is difficult to accomplish at the national level and will require external assistance to persuade governments to include climate change practitioners in their planning and development activities.

Enhancement of national and international partnerships is essential to ensure that all the competencies required for addressing climate change problems are available (WMO 2006). Universities are particularly important partners because much of the expertise on climate risk and development resides there. Improvement of the reliability of climate change information and, in particular, climate impact assessments should also be encouraged. The scientific community will need to make a concerted effort to develop the scientific and technical skills for better understanding of the effect of climate change on future weather risks, which, in turn, will enable more robust risk reduction strategies.

Conclusion

Climate change is one of the biggest risks facing society. Its effect on development and development investment may be the single most important factor undermining poverty reduction strategies. Development activities are particularly vulnerable because they are usually long term and are aimed at helping populations that are already exposed to greater relative risks because of their existing socioeconomic conditions: extreme poverty, food and water insecurity, and disease.

The impact of climate is unlikely to be incremental. More likely are changes in the character of existing natural hazards—storm surges, floods, droughts, and other extreme meteorological events. These risks must be understood and factored into development. The challenge for the global community is to enable developing countries to maintain an effective climate-monitoring network and climate change forecasting system that can help governments and donors assess the impact of climate change on development and include climate information in effective national disaster risk reduction strategies.

The nascent interest of the private sector in helping to sustain climate-observing networks needs to be encouraged, and every care must be taken to ensure that these new networks distribute their data widely, to everyone who wants it. Restrictions on access to and use of climate data should be avoided. Appropriate funding mechanisms must be found to retain the public goods ethos of climate information for development.

Notes

1. UKCIP Website, "Adaptation Wizard," http://www.ukcip.org.uk/index.php?option=com_content&task=view&id=147&Itemid=298.
2. See World Meteorological Organization, Commission on Climatology Web page, http://www.wmo.int/pages/prog/wcp/ccl/index_en.html.

References

Agrawala, Shardul, Simone Gigli, Vivian Raksakulthai, Andreas Hemp, Annett Moehner, Declan Conway, Mohamed El Raey, Ahsan Uddin Ahmed, James Risbey, Walter Barthgen, and Daniel Martino. 2005. "Climate Change and Natural Resource Management: Key Themes from Case Studies." In *Bridge over Troubled Waters: Linking Climate Change and Development*, ed. Shardul Agrawala, 85–132. Paris: Organisation for Economic Co-operation and Development (OECD) Publishing.

Bettencourt, Sofia, Richard Croad, Paul Freeman, John Hay, Roger Jones, Peter King, Padma Lal, Ala Mearns, Geoff Miller, Idah Pswarayi-Riddihough, Alf Simpson, Nakibae Teuatabo, Ulric Trotz, and Maarten van Aalst. 2006. "Not If, but When: Adapting to Natural Hazards in the Pacific Islands Region." Policy Note, World Bank, Washington, DC.

DFID (U.K. Department for International Development). 2006. "Reducing the Risks of Disasters—Helping to Achieve Sustainable Poverty Reduction in a Vulnerable World."

DFID Policy Paper, DFID, London. http://www.unisdr.org/news/DFID-reducing-risk-of-disasters.pdf.

GCOS (Global Climate Observing System). 2006. "Climate Information for Development Needs: An Action Plan for Africa. Report and Implementation Strategy, Addis Ababa, Ethiopia, 18–21 April 2006." GCOS 108, GCOS, Geneva. http://www.wmo.int/pages/prog/gcos/Publications/gcos-108%20%28ENGLISH%29.pdf.

GEF (Global Environment Facility). 2006. "Managing Climate Risk. Integrating Adaptation into World Bank Group Operations." World Bank, Washington, DC.

Ghebreyesus, T. A., Z. Tadese, D. Jima, E. Bekele, A. Mihretie, Y. Y. Yihdego, T. Dinku, S. J. Connor, and D. P. Rogers. 2008. "Public Health and Weather Services—Climate Information for the Health Sector." *WMO Bulletin* 57 (4, October): 256–61.

IFRC (International Federation of Red Cross and Red Crescent Societies). 2002. *World Disasters Report 2002: Focus on Reducing Risk.* Geneva: IFRC. http://www.ifrc.org/publicat/wdr/.

IRI (International Research Institute for Climate and Society). 2006. "A Gap Analysis for the Implementation of the Global Climate Observing Programme in Africa." IRI Technical Report, IRI-TR/06/1, IRI, Columbia University, New York.

Mogaka, Hezron, Sam Gichere, James Richard Davis, and Rafik Hirji. 2004. "Climate Variability in Kenya: Impacts and Responses." In "An Adaptation Mosaic: A Sample of the Emerging World Bank Work in Climate Change Adaptation. Final Draft," ed. Ajay Mathur, Ian Burton, and Maarten van Aalst, 71–82. World Bank Global Change Team, Washington, DC. http://siteresources.worldbank.org/INTCC/817372-1110879250911/20551573/AnAdaptationMosaicCCteam2004part1.pdf.

Munich Re. 2002. *Topics—Annual Review: Natural Catastrophes 2002.* Munich: Munich Re.

Rogers, D. P. 2007. "Weather, Climate, Water and Air Quality and the Risk to Development." In *Elements for Life*, 18–19. London: Tudor Rose for the World Meteorological Organization.

Rogers, David P., Mohammed Sadeck Boulahya, Madeleine C. Thomson, Stephen J. Connor, Tufa Dinku, Hany R. Shalaby, Babagana Ahmadu, and Abdoulah Niang. 2008. "Climate and Environmental Services for Development." In *International Symposium on Public Weather Services: A Key to Service Delivery (Geneva, 3–5 December 2007). Symposium Proceedings*, 88–93. WMO/TD-1438. Geneva: World Meteorological Organization. http://www.wmo.int/pages/prog/amp/pwsp/documents/Symposium_Proceedings_Final.pdf.

Smith, Joel B., Shardul Agrawala, Peter Larsen, and Frédéric Gagnon-Lebrun. 2005. "Climate Analysis." In *Bridge over Troubled Waters: Linking Climate Change and Development*, ed. Shardul Agrawala, 45–60. Paris: Organisation for Economic Co-operation and Development (OECD) Publishing.

Stern, Nicholas. 2007. *The Economics of Climate Change: The Stern Review.* Cambridge, U.K.: Cambridge University Press.

UNDP (United Nations Development Programme). 2004. *Reducing Disaster Risk: A Challenge for Development.* Global Report. New York: UNDP, Bureau for Crisis Prevention and Recovery. http://www.undp.org/cpr/whats_new/rdr_english.pdf.

United Nations. 2000. *United Nations Millennium Declaration.* General Assembly Resolution A/Res/55/2, September 18, United Nations, New York. http://www.un.org/millennium/declaration/ares552e.htm.

Washington, Richard, Mike Harrison, and Declan Conway. 2004. "African Climate Report: A Report Commissioned by the UK Government to Review African Climate Science, Policy and Options for Action." U.K. Department for Environment Food and Rural

Affairs (DEFRA) and U.K. Department for International Development (DFID), London. http://www.g7.utoronto.ca/environment/africa-climate.pdf.

WHO (World Health Organization). 2008a. *Closing the Gap in a Generation: Health Equity through Action on the Social Determinants of Health. Final Report of the Commission on Social Determinants of Health.* Geneva: WHO. http://whqlibdoc.who.int/publications/2008/9789241563703_eng.pdf.

———. 2008b. "Climate Change and Health." In "Sixty-First Session of the World Health Assembly, Geneva 19–24 May 2008, Resolutions and Decisions, Annexes." WHA61/2008/REC/1, WHO, Geneva. http://apps.who.int/gb/ebwha/pdf_files/WHA61-REC1/A61_REC1-en.pdf.

WMO (World Meteorological Organization). 2005. "Guidelines on Integrating Severe Weather Warnings in Disaster Risk Management." PWS-13, WMO/TD-1292, World Meteorological Organization, Geneva. http://www.wmo.int/pages/prog/amp/pwsp/pdf/TD-1292.pdf.

———. 2006. "Living with Climate Variability and Change: Understanding the Uncertainties and Managing the Risks." Conference Statement, Espoo, Finland, July 17–21, WMO, Geneva. http://www.wmo.int/pages/prog/wcp/wcasp/documents/WMO_Espoo_overview.pdf.

Part V
Financing Adaptation and
Mitigation in an Unequal World

International Climate Architecture and Financial Flows for Adaptation

CHARLOTTE STRECK

Climate change affects livelihoods, food security, and the economic output of developing countries. Although much of the attention in international negotiations is directed toward establishing emission reduction targets, for many developing countries, the priority response to climate change must be adaptation to its adverse effects. With changes in the climate becoming more prominent every year, adaptation is no longer just another policy option. Robust adaptation strategies to increase the climate resilience of local livelihoods and the domestic economy form an essential part of the response to climate change. Developing countries, however, often lack the means, technology, and institutional capacity to adapt effectively to changing climatic conditions and increased risks of extreme weather. These countries will need international support, as well as stable and predictable funding, to formulate policies and to build and establish national capacities.

This paper argues that adaptation efforts in developing countries should be supported by a multitude of funding sources, including funds mandated by the United Nations Framework Convention on Climate Change (UNFCCC) and bilateral sources. Developed-country contributions to those funds should be complemented by new forms of funding, such as a share of proceeds on carbon market transactions, a fee on bunker fuels, or other financing mechanisms. Adaptation needs to be an integrated part of a country's development policy, backed by official development assistance (ODA) and by national, multilateral, and dedicated climate funds supporting developing countries' transition toward climate-resilient economies.

Climate change affects livelihoods, food security, and the economic output of developing countries. Research shows that anomalously warm years reduce both the current level and the subsequent growth rate of gross domestic product (GDP),

Charlotte Streck is a founding partner and director of Climate Focus, Amsterdam, the Netherlands. The author thanks Carina Bracer and Mattia Fosci, who contributed to this chapter.

Berlin Workshop Series 2010

particularly in developing countries.[1] Similarly, evidence from Sub-Saharan Africa indicates that rainfall variability, which is projected to increase substantially, negatively affects GDP and increases poverty among rural communities (Brown et al. 2009). Other impacts expected from climate change include increased water scarcity and declining water quality; warming and acidification of the world's oceans; sea-level rise and the related coastal impacts; extreme weather events; climate-related impacts on public health; and additional threats to forest ecosystems and endangered species.

Developing countries often lack the means, technology, and institutional capacity to adapt effectively to changing climatic conditions and the increased risk of extreme weather. With changes in the climate becoming more prominent every year, adaptation is no longer optional; it becomes a necessity that has to be reflected in national policy making. The development of robust adaptation strategies to increase climate resilience forms an essential part of the national response to climate change. The effects of a changing climate are expected to be felt across all economic sectors and all social strata and social groups, heightening the need to understand the most effective adaptation measures and how best to implement them.

Discussions about the responsibilities for covering the costs of adaptation efforts, taking into account the impacts of climate change, have been ongoing since climate change negotiations began, but many questions remain unanswered, and the institutional structure for enhanced adaptation finance is still under negotiation. The international effort to promote adaptation has resulted in various initiatives, including the Nairobi Work Programme (2005–10), which was mandated by the Subsidiary Body for Scientific and Technical Advice (SBSTA) of the United Nations Framework Convention on Climate Change (UNFCCC) and which focuses on information sharing and learning among public, private, and civil society partners; the development of national adaptation programs of action (NAPAs) as a tool to help countries prioritize their adaptation needs; and the establishment of a specific adaptation fund. Decisions regarding the implementation of adaptation activities in the context of the UNFCCC take place under the Subsidiary Body for Implementation (SBI). Adaptation is also one of the four pillars of the Bali Action Plan, agreed on in 2007 by the 13th session of the Conference of the Parties (COP) to the UNFCCC. Discussions on enhanced action and international cooperation on adaptation "to enable and support the implementation of adaptation actions aimed at reducing vulnerability and building resilience in developing country Parties, especially in those that are particularly vulnerable" (FCCC/AWGLCA/2009/L.7/Rev.1 16 December 2009) are currently taking place within the contact group on adaptation of the UNFCCC's Ad Hoc Working Group on Long-Term Cooperative Action (AWG-LCA).

This chapter provides a brief overview of the needs for and sources of adaptation finance, followed by a description of potential future mechanisms for and sources of adaptation finance.

Financial Needs for Adaptation

The magnitude of financial needs for adaptation varies greatly, depending on the source and the method of estimating the scope of adaptation measures and on the time frame considered. Although there is general agreement that funding for addressing adaptation needs to be predictable, timely, adequate in size, appropriate in form, and equitable, there is no consensus on the amount of funds needed. Varying estimates exist of the economic, social, and environmental costs of the impacts of adaptation, and many of these are deemed incomplete or underestimated. Current attention and resources directed at preparing for and addressing adaptation are regarded as insufficient, and plans on how to address this situation remain vague.

The Stern Review (Stern 2007) calculated a need for between US$4 billion and US$37 billion per year between 2010 and 2015. Project Catalyst, an initiative of the ClimateWorks Foundation, estimates adaptation costs at US$14 billion to US$30 billion per year during the same period, just for knowledge development, disaster management, and planning. Commonly cited estimates conclude that by 2030, the additional investment needed globally for adaptation will be between US$49 billion and US$171 billion per year, of which US$28 billion to US$67 billion per year will be needed in developing countries (UNFCCC 2008). These figures have been challenged by a recent study conducted by the International Institute for Environment and Development (IIED), which reassessed cost estimates for, among other things, the housing and infrastructure sector, projected to be about US$315 billion per year by 2030, and ecosystem protection, estimated at US$60 billion to US$300 billion per year (Parry et al. 2009). Extending the projection beyond the 2030 deadline, the IIED study suggested that adaptation could cost up to US$9 trillion per year by 2060.

Developing countries that engage in adaptation planning (a) identify in their NAPAs those sectors in which intervention will likely be necessary, (b) prioritize projects, and (c) roughly quantify the funding involved. Contributions to quantifying the magnitude of finance needed are emerging via the United Nations–hosted Least Developed Country Portal—in particular, its NAPA Project Database, which presents ranked priority adaptation activities and projects of the (currently, 42) countries that have submitted an adaptation program of action. The amounts range from a US$100,000 project in Cambodia to provide safe water in regions at high risk of malaria to a US$23 million project in Bangladesh to reduce the risk of flooding through coastal afforestation, with community participation. Many of the estimates focus on expected infrastructure-related investments for adapting to climate impacts. Few include broader policy reforms to ensure that adequate institutions are put in place.

Sources of Finance for Adaptation

Financing for adaptation will have to come from a mix of national and international, public and private, funds. National costs of adaptation will be supported by international voluntary and commitment-based contributions. Nongovernmental organizations

(NGOs) and private sources, together with public bilateral and multilateral transfers, will finance adaptation activities.

UNFCCC funding covers the "additional costs" of adaptation—costs superimposed on vulnerable countries to meet their immediate adaptation needs, as opposed to "incremental costs," which are paid by the Global Environment Facility (GEF) in projects that generate global benefits.[2] The level of national financial commitments for adaptation depends on the development level and capabilities of each nation. The integration of adaptation activities into national plans and programs means that, at a minimum, national governments in least developed countries will finance both the groundwork preceding implementation of the proposed projects and the adequate involvement of unskilled workforces and local communities. Most important, it means that they will bear the residual economic costs of adaptation falling beyond the overall budget, provided that there is no additional international funding (i.e., within or outside the United Nations system).

The Conference of the Parties of the UNFCCC, at its seventh session, invited the GEF, as the financial mechanism of the convention, to establish and operate two new funds related to the convention: a Special Climate Change Fund (decision 7/CP.7, para. 2) and a Least Developed Countries Fund (para. 6). It also established a new fund related to the Kyoto Protocol, the Adaptation Fund, to be financed by a "share of the proceeds" of Clean Development Mechanism (CDM) project activities, as envisaged by article 12 of the Kyoto Protocol, and by additional funding invited from those Annex I parties intending to ratify the protocol (decision 10/CP.7, para. 2). Although the conference did not provide full guidance on these funds, the COP decision did lay down certain types of activities that might be financed by them.

The Adaptation Fund

The Adaptation Fund under the Kyoto Protocol was established to finance adaptation projects and programs in developing countries that are parties to the protocol. It is exclusively dedicated to the funding of concrete adaptation activities (Müller and Winkler 2008). The fund is replenished primarily from the proceeds of the 2 percent levy on transactions under the CDM but may be complemented by other sources of funding. An Adaptation Fund Board was created in 2007 (decision 1/CMP.3) as the operating entity of the Adaptation Fund. The board is fully accountable to the Conference of the Parties serving as the meeting of the parties to the Kyoto Protocol (CMP). On an interim basis, and subject to review every three years, the GEF was invited to serve as secretariat to the board, and the World Bank was invited to serve as trustee of the fund. Unlike the UNFCCC's Least Developed Countries Fund and the Special Climate Change Fund, the Adaptation Fund falls under the Kyoto Protocol. This implies that the fund is outside the sphere of the political influence of the United States, which has not ratified the protocol. Consequently, the European Union has been able to take a stronger leadership role for the developed countries in negotiating the operational aspects of the fund (Müller 2007).

By its decision 5/CMP.2 of 2006, the CMP agreed on a set of principles for the functioning of the Adaptation Fund. These principles include

- Balanced and equitable access to the fund
- Funding of the full (and not incremental) adaptation cost
- Accountability in the management, operation, and use of funds
- Short and efficient project development and approval cycles, and expedited processing of eligible activities
- The need for projects to be country driven, taking into account existing national planning exercises and development activities.

Considerable attention has been given to the governance and management of the Adaptation Fund, both within and outside the Kyoto Protocol negotiation process, primarily because of its uniqueness as a model for governance of climate change funding.

- To avoid a deficit of control that many developing countries felt with respect to the GEF-administered funds, a one-country, one-vote rule was made, and developing countries were accorded majority representation on the Adaptation Fund Board. The Board is composed of 16 members. Ten are from the five United Nations regional groups (two members each), one is from the group of small island developing states, one is from the least developed countries (LDCs), two are from the group of parties to Annex I of the UNFCCC (developed countries), and two are from those parties not included in Annex I (that is, from developing countries). Board decisions are taken by consensus, but if no agreement is reached, decisions are made by a two-thirds majority of the members present at the meeting, on the basis of one member, one vote.
- The CMP further decided in Bali that parties should have direct access to the Adaptation Fund, unlike the GEF-run funds. In line with decision 1/CMP.3, applicants to the Adaptation Fund can access funding either through a national executing entity ("direct access") or through an international implementing entity recognized by the Adaptation Fund Board. This was viewed as a victory for the developing world in moving toward creation of a new governance system for funding adaptation activities.

The Special Climate Change Fund

Pursuant to decision 7/CP.7, para. 2, the Special Climate Change Fund (SCCF) will be available for financing activities, programs, and measures relating to climate change that are complementary to those funded by the resources allocated to the climate change focal area of the GEF and by bilateral and multilateral sources. The SCCF is limited to the following areas: (a) adaptation (under decision 5/CP.7, para. 8); (b) technology transfer (decision 4/CP.7); (c) energy, transport, industry, agriculture, forestry, and waste management; and (d) in accordance with decision 5/CP.7, activities to assist developing country parties referred to in article 4, para. 8(h) in diversifying their economies; these are countries whose economies are highly dependent on income generated from the production, processing, and export of fossil fuels and associated energy-intensive products or on the consumption of these fuels and products.

Least Developed Countries Fund

Decision 7/CP.7 contains initial guidance on the Least Developed Countries (LDC) Fund, as a first step toward (a) providing funding from the LDC Fund to meet the agreed full cost of preparing NAPAs, which in turn will help build capacity for the preparation of national communications under article 12, para. 1, of the UNFCCC; (b) ensuring complementarity of funding between the LDC Fund and other funds with which the operating entity is entrusted; (c) ensuring the separation of the LDC Fund from other funds with which the operating entity is entrusted; (d) adopting simplified procedures and arranging for expedited access to the fund by the least developed countries while ensuring sound financial management; (e) ensuring transparency in all steps relating to the operation of the fund; (f) encouraging the use of national and, where appropriate, regional experts; (g) adopting streamlined procedures for the operation of the fund.

In addition to these funds, the GEF operates the Strategic Operational Approach to Adaptation. With a budget of only US$313 million, the three GEF-managed funds (the Least Developed Countries Fund, the SCCF, and the Strategic Operational Approach to Adaptation) provide hardly a drop in the bucket of adaptation finance needs. Adding in the numerous bilateral and other multilateral initiatives brightens the picture somewhat.[3] Yet, at about US$1 billion per year (Ghosh and Woods 2009), including transfers under the UNFCCC, current transfers for adaptation still fall short of even the most conservative estimates of financing needs. Pending the outcome of U.S. Senate deliberations on future climate legislation, significant further adaptation funding may become available. The American Clean Energy and Security Act (Waxman-Markey), for example, would have made available 5 percent of the revenues received by the U.S. government from auctioning permits for adaptation and technology transfer in developing countries (Stewart, Kingsbury, and Rudyk 2009).

Tracking additional sources and flows of finance for adaptation is the goal of the Web-based UN Adaptation Funding Interface, which was created in compliance with a decision by the SBI at the 10th COP. Parties seeking financial contributions for actions, or donors accepting requests for support, can use this Web site to find a match for their needs.

Adaptation Finance Outlook

New sources of finance need to be accessed in order to support developing countries' needs for adaptation finance. There is a wide range of proposals on how new and additional international resources could be mobilized. Developing countries stress the need for public sector contributions from industrial nations as the main form of finance, while the latter highlight the importance of private financing and market-linked mechanisms as key funding sources. The current UNFCCC financial mechanism is supported by voluntary contributions from developed countries. China has proposed that developed countries commit 0.5 percent of their total GDP to support projects addressing climate change in developing countries. India argues similarly and proposes a GDP-dependent contribution from Annex I countries of 0.3 to 1.0 percent; private financing would be welcome, but merely as an additional contribution. Such targets are, however, as vulnerable as current funding commitments for development aid—as exemplified by the problems in enforcing the official development assistance (ODA) target of 0.7 percent of gross national income, set in 2002 at the Conference on Development Financing in Monterrey, Mexico. South Africa advocates a blend of sources: Annex I public contributions, marked linked shares from the auctioning of allowances, and the carbon market. Among developing countries, the most differentiated proposal is that of Mexico, for a financial model under which all countries except the least developed would contribute in accordance with their respective historic responsibility, actual greenhouse gas quotas, GDP, and population.

Annex I countries are generally less outspoken on the sources of funding. The European Union is open to discussing various sources of funding. Examples include government contributions by countries; international auctioning of internationally assigned emission quotas (such as assigned amount units, or AAUs); and levies on international aviation and maritime transport. The most pronounced proposals come from Switzerland and Norway. Switzerland envisages a global carbon tax of US$2 per ton of carbon dioxide equivalent (tCO2e) on all fossil fuel emissions; developing countries below a certain level of GDP per capita would be excluded. Norway's plan merges public funding sources with private-style sourcing through international auctions of AAUs.

Although developed countries have to live up to their promise to make financing available to support adaptation efforts, developing countries have to engage in strategic planning and implementation to integrate adaptation into their national development plans. Support from industrial countries for developing countries is essential so that the latter can

- *Develop and implement country-specific integrated mitigation and adaptation (low-carbon development) strategies.* Funding for policy development is essential to ensure that African countries can develop informed climate and carbon strategies.
- *Promote further research, data collection, and institutional strengthening.* Few developing countries currently have the experience and capacity to assess climate impacts on the ground. Research, technical assistance, technology transfer, and capacity building are essential for the accurate accounting of carbon and for the building of local centers of excellence.
- *Finance programs and project activities.* Funding is essential for the adoption of government programs that support much-needed investments. It is further needed to stimulate private investments on the ground by providing technical assistance for the development of adaptation projects and programs.

Developing countries will need stable and predictable funding to formulate policies and to build and establish national capacities. A funding mechanism that channels resources to developing-country economies as soon as possible is therefore essential. Funding for institutional expenses and budget lines should be supported by multilateral sources that could be replenished from a share of proceeds on carbon market transactions, a fee on bunker fuels, or other finance mechanisms. Since market-based mechanisms such as carbon trading are unlikely to support adaptation finance, it will be more difficult to attract private funding and investment into adaptation than into mitigation measures (Gomez-Echeverri 2009, 167). Therefore, adaptation needs to become part of a country's general development policy, backed by ODA and by national, multilateral, and dedicated climate funds supporting developing countries' transition toward climate-resilient economies.

Notes

1. For an analysis of the relationship between development and climate change, see *World Development Report 2010*, ch. 1 (http://siteresources.worldbank.org/INTWDR2010/Resources/5287678-1226014527953/Chapter-1.pdf).
2. FCCC/AWGLCA/2008/INF.2, November 19, 2008.
3. Industrial countries provide funding for adaptation activities via multilateral entities such as the World Bank (e.g., Pilot Programme for Climate Resilience, US$240 million) and the European Commission (European Commission Global Climate Change Alliance, US$84 million over three years; European Union proposal within the Blueprint for Copenhagen of US$21 billion until 2021) or directly through bilateral arrangements. Examples of the latter are the Japanese Cool Earth Partnership (US$1 billion) and the United Nations Development Programme (UNDP)–Spain Millennium Development Goal (MDG) Achievement Fund (US$22 million for five years).

References

Brown, Casey, Robyn Meeks, Yonas Ghile, and Kenneth Hunu. 2009. "An Empirical Analysis of Effects of Climate Variables on National Level Economic Growth." Background paper for *World Development Report 2010*, World Bank, Washington, DC.

Ghosh, Arunabha, and Ngaire Woods. 2009. "Developing Country Concerns about Climate Finance Proposals: Priorities, Trust, and the Credible Donor Problem." In *Climate Finance: Regulatory and Funding Strategies for Climate Change and Global Development,* ed. Richard B. Stewart, Benedict Kingsbury, and Bryce Rudyk, 157–64. New York: New York University Press.

Gomez-Echeverri, Luis. 2009. "Developing Countries and a Proposal for Architecture and Governance of a Reformed UNFCCC Financial Mechanism." In *Climate Finance: Regulatory and Funding Strategies for Climate Change and Global Development,* ed. Richard B. Stewart, Benedict Kingsbury, and Bryce Rudyk, 165–71. New York: New York University Press.

Müller, Benito. 2007. "The Nairobi Climate Change Conference: A Breakthrough for Adaptation Funding." Oxford Energy and Environment Comment, January, Oxford Institute for Energy Studies, Oxford, U.K. http://www.oxfordenergy.org/pdfs/comment_0107-1.pdf.

Müller, Benito, and Harald Winkler. 2008. "One Step Forward, Two Steps Back? The Governance of the World Bank Climate Investment Funds." Oxford Energy and Environment Comment, February 2008, Oxford Institute for Energy Studies, Oxford, U.K. http://www.oxfordenergy.org/pdfs/comment_0208-1.pdf.

Parry, Martin, Nigel Arnell, Pam Berry, David Dodman, Samuel Fankhauser, Chris Hope, Sari Kovats, Robert Nicholls, David Sattherwaite, Richard Tiffin, and Tim Wheeler. 2009. *Assessing the Costs of Adaptation to Climate Change: A Critique of the UNFCCC Estimates.* London: International Institute for Environment and Development (IIED) and Grantham Institute for Climate Change, Imperial College London.

Stern, Nicholas. 2007. *The Economics of Climate Change: The Stern Review.* Cambridge, U.K.: Cambridge University Press.

Stewart, Richard B., Benedict Kingsbury, and Bryce Rudyk, eds. 2009. *Climate Finance: Regulatory and Funding Strategies for Climate Change and Global Development.* New York: New York University Press.

UNFCCC (United Nations Framework Convention on Climate Change). 2008. "Investment and Financial Flows to Address Climate Change." UNFCCC Secretariat, Bonn, Germany.

World Bank. 2009. *World Development Report 2010: Development and Climate Change.* Washington, DC: World Bank.

Part VI
Changing Climate, Changing Institutions of Governance

Creating the Capacity for Decentralized, Self-Governing Adaptations to Climate Change

JOHN SCANLON AND CLARA NOBBE

Findings by the Intergovernmental Panel on Climate Change tell us that adaptation has become as important a response to climate change as mitigation. In fact, failure to take effective adaptation measures will threaten the achievement of most of the United Nations Millennium Development Goals and will have severe implications for the well-being of populations throughout the world.

This paper focuses on the water-related impacts of climate change, which will disproportionately affect already vulnerable groups, particularly in developing countries. It acknowledges the challenges associated with effective adaptation—in particular, the need for additional investments, technological development, and an extended science base—but it also sees opportunities for tackling the adaptation challenge by integrating adaptive measures into existing governance systems. Effective adaptation will require greater emphasis on local solutions, including the strengthening of local governance structures.

The Fourth Assessment Report of the Intergovernmental Panel on Climate Change (IPCC) presents various scenarios of climate change for the unfolding century. The severity of the impacts corresponds to increases in global mean temperature, but with regional variations. An increase of 0.2°C in temperature is projected per decade over the next two decades, followed by a variety of possible scenarios. These range from a temperature increase of 0.6°C to one of 4.0°C, depending on the level of concentration of greenhouse gases (GHGs) and aerosols at any specific time until the end of this century (IPCC 2007, 7). For the purposes of this analysis, it is assumed that neither the worst-case nor the best-case scenario will occur.

John Scanlon is principal adviser on policy and program to the executive director of the United Nations Environment Programme. Clara Nobbe is associate program officer at the United Nations Environment Programme.

Berlin Workshop Series 2010
© 2010 The International Bank for Reconstruction and Development / The World Bank

In line with the IPCC findings, the consequences of climate change can already be observed at the global level in the melting of snow, ice, and frozen ground in mountain areas and the polar regions; changes in hydrological systems, including runoff and thermal structures; and poleward and upward shifts in plant and animal ranges in terrestrial systems. At the regional level, changes in the Northern Hemisphere in agriculture and forestry management, human health, and human activities in the Arctic are other likely effects of climate change (IPCC 2007, 2). The projected global impacts include a significant loss of biodiversity; severe effects on water availability and related impacts on food security; the spread of arid and semiarid regions, with implications for food production; sea-level rise and associated risks to coastal communities; increases in the frequency and severity of extreme weather events; and growing health risks (IPCC 2007, 11).

The projected impacts of climate change are exacerbating current stresses such as threats to water security; the overexploitation of other natural resources (in particular, forest and marine resources); the effects of land-based sources of pollution on the marine environment; and the removal of natural sea defenses such as mangroves. Not only are the impacts of climate change exacerbating existing stresses; already vulnerable regions are being and will be confronted with multiple stresses.

Mitigation measures are essential for managing levels of concentration of GHGs and aerosols, as a means of managing rises in temperature. However, the above-cited evidence of the climate change that is already being experienced, and the exacerbation of existing stresses, demand investment in the development of adaptation measures, as well. Water security, as one of the most basic, yet interrelated, requirements for human life and sustainable development, provides a compelling topic of analysis, especially in relation to governance.

The paper explores the options and requirements for effective, decentralized governance systems that will facilitate adaptation to the impacts of climate change on freshwater security. Following an outline of the water-related impacts of climate change, the paper investigates the main prerequisites for adaptation: changes in governance and institutions, additional investment, greater collaboration between the science community and policy makers, and technological development. It concludes by arguing that effective adaptation requires more emphasis on local solutions, including the strengthening of local governance structures.

Adaptation and the Water Priority

Water has a central role in our life support system. The main challenges associated with freshwater are that there is too much of it, or too little of it, or that it is polluted. All these problems can be exacerbated by climate change. Water resources are further affected by many nonclimatic drivers, including human activities such as agriculture, land-use change, infrastructure, pollutant emissions, and wastewater treatment; by demographic changes; by socioeconomic development and changing food patterns; and by policies and regulations.

Socioeconomic Challenges for Water Resource Management

Water analyses accordingly need to make a distinction between socioeconomic or general environmental changes and modifications of water resources related to climate change. In relation to the first category, the IPCC has observed a global increase in water use because of rapid rates of population growth and an increase in the use of irrigation water, including its employment in irrigation-based agriculture. It has identified a number of water-stressed basins in, among other areas, northern Africa, the Mediterranean region, the Middle East, the Near East, southern Asia, northern China, Australia, the United States, Mexico, northeastern Brazil, and the west coast of South America.[1] Equally related to socioeconomic drivers is a general decline in water quality as a consequence of increased agricultural and industrial activity (IPCC 2008, 8). Future projections foresee a further increase in water consumption as a result of population growth and increased irrigation.[2] Water quality will continue to be compromised by toxic effluents, as the use of nutrients and pesticides is expected to grow in developing countries, rendering improvements in wastewater treatment negligible (IPCC 2008, 10).

Climate Change Challenges for Water Resource Management

Although climate change impacts will be experienced differently depending on region, the IPCC predicts that the overall impacts of climate change on water resources will have negative implications and will generally aggravate existing water stresses. These facts provide a basis for addressing the adaptation challenge.

The effects of global warming on water resources can be seen in the increased melting of mountain glaciers, snow cover, and frozen ground, resulting in changes in river flows. Mountains, acting as natural water towers, store water as ice and snow during the winter and gradually release it during the summer. The rise in global temperatures will lead to increased glacial melting. At first, the result will be increased flows, but as glaciers disappear, flows will be reduced, causing, first, floods and then droughts. Increased river flows can already be observed in the Andes and the Alps, and earlier spring peak flows have been found in North America and Eurasia (IPCC 2008, 35).

Whereas the impacts of changes in temperature on rainfall are well understood, it is less clear how temperature changes affect the availability of water from rivers, lakes, and underground sources. What is known is that higher temperatures will increase evaporation, which, if not offset by rainfall, will increase aridity. Aridity, in turn, will have negative effects on both surface water runoff and groundwater recharge.

Rises in temperature will also lead to the deterioration of water quality because of pollution by sediments, nutrients, and pesticides caused by low water levels stemming from changing precipitation patterns. Other phenomena are increased water erosion and sedimentation caused by increased runoff, as snow is replaced by rainfall, and decreased water quality as a result of the intrusion of seawater into coastal freshwater systems.

Despite recognition of the importance of monitoring changes in the hydrological cycle, the development of monitoring systems and the maintenance of databases have remained limited (GWP 2008, 4). Thus, little information is available to policy makers for making informed planning decisions, whether in developing or developed countries.

The Larger Picture

The consequences of climate change are also felt in other water-using sectors and systems, with implications for countries' broader economic, social, and environmental variables, particularly in poorer societies. In fact, since water resource management is essential to the achievement of the Millennium Development Goals (MDGs), these impacts will jeopardize their realization.

In the agricultural sector, climate-related impacts on water resources have critical implications for food security, poverty alleviation, and sustainable development. With 80 percent of global agricultural land being rainfed, variations in temporal and spatial rainfall heavily determine the productivity of the sector. Marginal lands face even greater challenges with respect to water. Given increased water stress, irrigation, which is currently applied to 18 percent of global agricultural land, is not a sustainable solution. Food security is further threatened by projected increases in climate variability and droughts, with impacts on grassland productivity and negative implications for livestock farming. Areas particularly affected are South America, southern and northern Africa, western Asia, Australia, and southern Europe (GWP 2008, 60).

Water scarcity, exacerbated by climate change, is projected to affect human health, in particular by increasing malnutrition and thus rendering populations more vulnerable to, and less capable of coping with, diseases. Drinking-water quality is expected to be directly and indirectly compromised as a result of an increase in extreme weather events. Vectorborne diseases are expected to increase as changes in climate expand the spatial distribution of vectors (GWP 2008, 67ff).

The effects of climate change on water also have implications for human settlements and infrastructure. The impact will vary according to socioeconomic development, geographic location, the existence of infrastructure, and institutional development. The water sector itself will, in water-stressed regions, be increasingly challenged to keep up with provision of high-quality water, infrastructure development, maintenance, and regulation.

The main impact of climate change in many sectors may be an increase in the costs of water services and delivery. In particular, ecosystem water use will experience extreme pressure as costs of water rise. Because few countries have effective measures in place to ensure adequate water for ecosystems, that water is often the first to be diverted.

Global trade in water-intensive products ("virtual water") may increase as water availability at the country level changes. This should result in changed trade patterns, with a shift of water-intensive exports to water-rich areas.

The observed and projected impacts of climate change on the water sector are vast. Given the extent to which change has occurred already, and the magnitude of changes foreseen in the short-to-medium-term future, mitigation measures would take too long to become effective, thus shifting action in the water sector toward adaptation. Moreover, the water-related impacts of climate change will disproportionately affect already vulnerable groups, mostly in developing countries, whose governments have neither the primary responsibility for the occurrence of climate change nor the means to take mitigation action.

The interrelationships between the water sector and other sectors, with the consequent uncertainties as to how and to what degree changes in one sector affect another, mandate an integrated approach toward the management of water resources. Globally observed phenomena often take on very specific features at the local level and require responses that cater to local needs. The adaptation challenge thus requires that additional effort be focused on integrated management of resources at the catchment and river basin levels through such means as new or enhanced governance arrangements.

Greater investment in adaptation provides an opportunity for building more enduring capacity to manage freshwater and other natural resources, which in turn will prompt positive spillover effects on areas such as food production and infrastructure.

In light of the significance of water for many sectors of society, the Global Water Partnership has suggested that it be given the same attention and focus within adaptation efforts that energy receives in mitigation action (GWP 2008, 2).

Adaptation Needs

Mitigation measures seek to reduce emissions of GHGs and halt climate change. *Adaptation* to climate change has been defined by the United Nations Framework Convention on Climate Change (UNFCCC) as "taking the right measures to reduce the negative effects of climate change (or exploit the positive ones) by making the appropriate adjustments and changes." It is "a process through which societies make themselves better able to cope with an uncertain future" (UNFCCC 2007, 12).

Climate variability has always required people to adapt to different conditions. The concept of adaptation is thus not new; it has been applied by local communities and farmers all over the world. Yet the scale of climate change we face today and expect to experience in the future requires a much broader response. To meet the adaptation challenge, there is a need for

- A new approach to governance and the reform of institutions, including broader participation in decision-making processes and accountability
- Additional investment
- Closer cooperation between the science and policy communities
- Further development of technology.

Governance and Institutional Reform

Adaptation, as a response to the impacts of climate change, cuts across all sectors of the economy and society. This means that, at the international level, there is a need to improve collaboration among specialized agencies and multilateral development banks to foster the coherence of their interventions. The environment, as one of the key components of sustainable development, needs to be recognized as the foundation of the economic and social pillars. This approach lays down a conceptual basis for mainstreaming adaptation into the different program areas of the various specialized agencies.

Organizations specifically responsible for the environment, in particular the United Nations Environment Programme, need to be strengthened to enable them to fulfill their mandates more effectively. As part of the governance system, the profiles of multilateral environmental agreements (MEAs), whose implementation contributes significantly to climate change adaptation, need to be enhanced and their interlinkages with other international legal agreements reassessed.

At the national level, effective adaptation requires both vertical and horizontal integration of all relevant sectors and a simultaneous top-down and bottom-up approach to ensure that any policy is matched by the necessary adaptive capacity of each stakeholder to implement it. This means that sectors that have previously operated in isolation will need to cooperate and develop joint policies and action plans. For example, at the horizontal level, ministries of finance or economics need to collaborate closely with ministries of environment, agriculture, energy, and social affairs to ensure that their policies consider the interlinkages between, for example, water scarcity, its social impacts, the implications for economic development, and the financing of any remedial action. At the vertical level, this would require national bodies to work closely with regional and local authorities, as well as with the local community (including indigenous peoples, where relevant), nongovernmental organizations (NGOs), and the private sector to ensure the broadest participation and the inclusion of the widest range of stakeholders in the decision-making process.

Adjusting governance structures to meet the adaptation challenge further necessitates institutional reforms. Institutional functions that must be geared toward the adaptation challenge include the mobilization, allocation, and disbursement of funds; policy and strategy formulation; knowledge and information management; implementation; and accountability. Because of a lack of capacity, institutions in developing countries, in particular, are often unable to fulfill these basic functions.

Creating a better governance system for water is essential, given the magnitude of the adaptation challenge. In fact, the water crisis is increasingly being described as a governance crisis (Plummer and Slaymaker 2007, 3) because of the fragmentation of rules and laws, authorities, and relationships between actors in the water sector at both the international and national levels. Given its cross-sectoral relevance, water management, broadly defined, requires a much more comprehensive approach than is currently taken—an approach that integrates all water-using sectors, including ecosystem management, coastal systems, agriculture and forestry, industry, sanitation, and the health sector. This idea is captured in the concept of integrated water resources management (IWRM), which was laid out at the Rio Earth Summit in 1992.[3]

IWRM provides a set of tools and standards to guide governments in managing water resources. Both hard and soft measures are recommended—the former relating to the development of infrastructure, such as the construction of dams, canals, and pipelines, and the latter to the development of policies on water allocation, conservation, and efficiency; rules on ownership, land use, and changes in land use; and instruments for managing demand, such as pricing mechanisms. However, a survey conducted by the United Nations World Water Assessment Programme (WWAP) in 2008 shows that most of the 104 countries that responded to the survey had not fully implemented their IWRM plans (WWAP 2009, 243), mainly because of insufficient funds and capacity. Even if it is sufficiently resourced and implemented, IWRM does not solve the governance challenge of the water sector. Although it establishes high technical standards and methodologies, it fails to take account of the political aspects of water resource management, such as participatory democracy, transparency, and accountability (Plummer and Slaymaker 2007, 4).

As part of an effective governance system, there is a need to create "intelligent institutions" in the water sector. Because of the political significance of water, most countries have long-established authorities that deal with it. The monopolistic nature of the sector, however, often means that water authorities are lethargic toward modernization and show tendencies toward corrupt behavior. The creation of intelligent institutions—institutions "that can go beyond managing water on a day to day basis to identify water use trends, areas vulnerable to climate change and opportunities to respond as best possible to the emerging challenges" (GWP 2007, 8)—is thus critical.

Investment

There is a real risk that climate change will impede the achievement of the MDGs. Success in lowering or averting the risk implies higher investment in adaptation measures and, in fact, requires funds beyond traditional commitments for overseas development assistance (ODA). The estimated costs of adaptation range between US$3 billion and US$135 billion per year, based on assessments produced during 2006–8 (ClimateWorks Foundation 2009). The UNFCCC, in a 2008 assessment, estimated that "overall additional investment and financial flows needed for adaptation in 2030 amounted to several tens and possibly hundreds, of billions of United States dollars" (UNFCCC 2008, 22). All estimates agree that the costs of adaptation are lower than the costs of potential impacts. Given the significant differences in estimates, it has been recommended that each country develop its own national "Stern Review"—a reference to the much-quoted report by Nicholas Stern (CCCD 2009a, 34; see Stern 2007).

Recognition of the need for additional investment does not translate into availability of funds. Developing countries argue that investment in adaptation must be separate from and additional to ODA, but developed countries have failed to honor their pledge to allocate 0.7 percent of gross national income (GNI) to ODA. Financing mechanisms under the Global Environment Facility (GEF), the UNFCCC, and the World Bank are insufficient for meeting investment needs. Moreover, existing funding mechanisms are inefficient because of their incoherent setup, incurring high transaction costs. Hence, alternatives are currently being discussed in the run-up to the UNFCCC Copenhagen conference, focusing on national budgetary allocations, national market-based levies, and international market-based levies. No matter what the international community comes up with in the shape of new financing arrangements, it is crucial for the effectiveness of the undertaking that funding be both coherent and predictable.

In ensuring the effectiveness of multilateral financing mechanisms, there is an urgent need to apply the principles of ownership, alignment, harmonization, management for results, and mutual accountability (as set out in the Paris Declaration on Aid Effectiveness and elaborated on in the follow-up Accra Agenda for Action) during the establishment and disbursement of funds. A recent study shows that implementation of the declaration is still lacking, in all areas (OECD DAC 2009).

In light of the amount of resources needed to meet the adaptation challenge, the role of and opportunities for the private sector should not be underestimated. Whether public-private partnerships or purely private investments are involved, governments must create the necessary incentives and regulations to ensure the private sector's participation in adaptation actions.

The financing of adaptation in the water sector is in itself a challenge, as the sector has suffered from chronic lack of political support, poor governance, underresourcing, and underinvestment (WWAP 2009, 57). Costs associated with water management can be split into three categories: (a) resource management and development, including watershed and river basin management, storage, flood-risk management, pollution abatement, and environmental protection; (b) services to municipalities and households, agriculture, and industry, including wastewater treatment and operation and maintenance of infrastructure; and (c) integrative functions, including policy development and legislation, research, monitoring, administration, and public information. Effective adaptation requires further investment in all these categories, as conditions are projected to become even more severe under the impact of climate change.

The financing of adaptation has to recognize the importance of a healthy water sector to the functioning of other sectors and so should take into consideration a broad range of financing sources. With respect to existing and planned international financing mechanisms, there is a need to investigate the possible multiplier effects that could be realized by focusing investment on the water sector. A similar rationale applies to national sources of financing, such as public expenditures and user tariffs. Here, there needs to be an emphasis on equitable solutions, including application of the polluter-pays principle and incrementally rising "luxury" fees for the use of water above a certain quantity.

Science-Policy Interface

Effective policies need to be informed by sound science. Even though scientific knowledge about climate change is expanding quickly, the links between scientific institutions and policy makers remain weak, inhibiting policy makers' capacity to make educated choices as to where and how to take adaptive measures.

In relation to water, there is a need to expose the interlinkages between climate change and food, energy (biofuels), and water security; the impacts of climate change on ecosystems; and the implications for human health. Despite the benefits of information collection and exchange at the global level for observing general trends, effective water policies and planning at the local level are dependent on research into local circumstances. This requires greater collaboration between climate change experts, national and local water authorities, and regional planners in order to feed information on local conditions into local planning. In particular, information concerning the impacts of climate change on local water quality and water storage opportunities and an assessment of water rights and allocation would enhance adaptation planning.

In the area of disaster management, studies have shown that collaboration between disaster managers, local authorities, and scientists that yields insights into key drivers of climate events has a positive impact on disaster preparedness and response. By producing, managing, and disseminating knowledge, governments can greatly enhance citizens' capacity to take individual adaptive action and can significantly reduce the impacts of disasters.

Technology

Facilitation of adaptation also requires technological innovation and the availability of technologies to the public at large. Because it is often the poorest who are the most vulnerable, mechanisms have to be found to enable the transfer of technology at affordable prices to these segments of society.

In relation to adaptation in the water sector, technology plays a crucial role. There are two aspects to the challenge. On the one hand, water technology must be adjusted to meet the needs of adaptation. This requires that it be well informed by climate science, in order for dams, canals, pipelines, wastewater treatment plants, stormwater drainage systems, and other water-related infrastructure to be built with the ability to withstand the impacts of climate change (GWP 2007, 9). On the other hand, technology needs to be affordable, as those in need are often those least in a position to acquire it.

Although adaptation measures benefit from international experience, successful adaptation is, quintessentially, a matter of finding local solutions. Governance systems need to be adjusted to local requirements, as well as informed by science;

financing solutions will greatly depend on local circumstances; and technological adjustments will follow local needs.

Adaptation and Local Solutions: Building on Existing Strategies

Climate change impacts differ according to region and therefore require diverse adaptation measures. Whereas certain regions will see increased incidences of precipitation and flooding, others will experience more frequent spells of dry periods and drought. Although the adaptation needs described above are generally observed requirements, they will vary in their intensity depending on existing local structures. Individuals and communities have always had to adapt to changing circumstances. Climate change adds another layer of risk to people's lives, but adaptive action needs to be understood as reinforcing ongoing development processes and strengthening existing governance structures (CCCD 2009b, 12).

In the context of water, this means understanding the impacts of changes in water supply on people's lives. These impacts include direct effects, such as loss of land to rising sea levels, flooding, and desertification, and indirect effects, such as diminished market opportunities for agricultural produce or marine resources as a result of the degradation of agricultural land or the marine environment. Adaptation measures need to be embedded in existing policies and programs that address these issues—for example, integrated water resource management, coastal defense and risk reduction strategies, and country development policies and programs, including poverty reduction strategy papers and sector policies.

Action at the local, subnational, and national levels will ensure that benefits accrue to the respective stakeholders. Subregional approaches will become increasingly important where transboundary water resources are concerned. Water scarcity increases the risk of conflict between states, and joint resource management can help lower that risk.

A useful guidance for governments in designing and implementing adaptive measures is the principle of subsidiarity, which states that measures should be taken at the lowest possible administrative level. Although the principle was not developed in connection with climate change action, it is becoming increasingly relevant to adaptation.

Adaptation and Powers, Functions, and Capacities

The ability to take adaptive measures will be influenced by existing capacities and governance arrangements. As described above, effective adaptation requires both horizontal and vertical integration of governance structures, decentralization, and an encompassing approach to governance, enabling NGOs, civil society, and the private sector to participate in decision making and in the establishment of an accountability framework.

How far this is possible will depend on the functions and power structures of ministries, local governments, and specialized bodies such as water and catchment authorities. A prerequisite for collaboration is a common recognition and understanding of the adaptation challenge by the various governing bodies, and that largely depends on their access to scientific information, including data and analysis from both international and national sources. Constraints on collaboration also arise as a result of overlapping of functions and powers between line ministries and between central and local governments. Because competition for funds between ministries is often endemic, the sharing of responsibilities is difficult to implement.

Decentralization and promotion of the leadership of local governments and authorities—the bodies best informed about local conditions—in devising and implementing adaptive measures are viewed as crucial in tackling the adaptation challenge in the water sector. Decentralization can also assist the establishment or enhancement of catchment or river basin bodies to manage freshwater and other natural resources. The creation of such bodies can help reduce political interests by transcending administrative boundaries and adopting a more integrative approach toward water resource management.

Decentralized governance approaches will benefit greatly from participation by civil society and NGOs in local water management. By advocating for action, helping to set the rules, and monitoring implementation, these bodies can act as important watchdogs to ensure that adaptive measures are taken. Civil society and NGOs can assist in filling the gap between national and local governments by providing multistakeholder platforms for discussions on how to address climate risk.

It is equally important to integrate the business community into decision-making processes in view of its role in commercial activities related to natural resource management. Tax revenues generated from the business sector can be an important source of financing for infrastructure.

Adaptation and Existing Challenges: Building Enduring Capacity

The concept that adaptation measures are most effective if planned within the local context and implemented by local actors presumes a certain amount of capacity on the part of stakeholders at all levels. The concept of capacity, which is borrowed from the development discourse, covers aspects of wealth, health, education and the knowledge needed for exercising judgment, and political influence. Adaptive capacity is thus related to "the opportunity to make adaptive choices, whether those choices are made, and the results when adaptive choices have been made" (CCCD 2009b, 14).

Successful adaptation requires that those affected by climate change be able to recognize, plan for, overcome, and reflect on challenges. Individuals and communities have often learned to cope with the impacts of climate change, but repeated coping usually leads them into a downward socioeconomic spiral and increases their vulnerability. Effective adaptation, by contrast, will increase resilience. It is, therefore, important that the building of adaptive capacity be integrated into ongoing capacity-building measures, given the interrelationship between adaptation and the existing need to manage natural resources more effectively.

Studies in Brazil and Niger show that the adaptive capacity of local communities can be greatly enhanced by strengthening and building on current local approaches (Tearfund 2008, 51). Interventions that were identified as benefiting from additional technical input and access to microcredit schemes include water harvesting and small storage facilities; small-scale, community-based irrigation schemes; and improved management of soil moisture in rainfed areas (Tearfund 2008, 52).

The need to enhance adaptive capacity arises not only with respect to local communities but also at the government level. "Intelligent institutions" are dependent on the capacities of those who run them, and integrative governance systems require able contributors.

Conclusions

Despite recognition of the importance of water for the achievement of the MDGs and the risk that the impacts of climate change on water resources will threaten their achievement, countries have yet to apply comprehensive adaptation measures to water resource management.

Needed for adaptation are an improved governance system and more flexible and proactive institutions, closer cooperation between science and policy makers, increased technological development, and, to facilitate all these, additional investment.

The IWRM approach provides a valuable conceptual framework for water resource management. Its shortcomings lie in its mainly technical approach, leaving out the political complexities that frequently arise. This paper suggests that the solution to effective water resource management can be found in the creation of decentralized governance systems, applying IWRM. Since the impacts of climate change are mostly felt at the local level, by local communities, this approach would enable local circumstances to be taken into account. In order to improve the transparency and accountability of water resource management bodies, the governance system should provide for the participation of a broad range of stakeholders, including civil society, NGOs, and the private sector.

Particularly in the context of watercourses that stretch across a country's international or administrative borders, further synergies could be created by establishing a governance system centered on catchment areas or river basins. The benefits of such an approach can be seen in the example of the Murray-Darling Basin Initiative in Australia (box 1).

The success of decentralized governance systems will depend greatly on the adaptive capacities of all the stakeholders involved. Evidence shows that although, throughout human history, local communities have developed capacities to adapt to climate variability, the current and future impacts of climate change require enhanced adaptive capacities of all stakeholders at all levels.

BOX 1. Adaptation and River Basin Management: A Case Study

The effective management of fresh water and other natural resources requires a catchment level or river basin approach that allows decisions to be made in an appropriate context and on an appropriate scale. The powers and functions to be conferred on such bodies are for governments and their communities to determine.

This approach will become increasingly important as local communities respond to the impacts of climate change—for example, increased incidence of drought or floods—and to the related issues of food production, infrastructure, migration, and policy (governance and regulation). It will need to be responsive to local conditions, and the starting point will vary according to local governance arrangements and capacity. The size and scale of the adaptation and the related capacity-building challenges are apparent from looking at the scope of the adaptation effort required in one of the best-recognized and longest-standing river basin organizations in the world, the Murray-Darling Basin Authority (formerly, Commission) in Australia.

The management of the water resources of the Murray-Darling Basin (MDB) benefits from more than a hundred years of experience with adaptive management. The responsible authority, the MDB Commission, was active in identifying and quantifying the risks to the water resources of the basin, including the risk posed by climate change. The responses to those risks have led to significant changes in how the basin is managed. These adjustments include

- Changes in governance arrangements, including the relationship between central and subnational governments, and reinforcement of catchment management authorities that bring together central, subnational, and local governments and the local community
- Significant additional investment in the basin, in the order of $A13 billion over 10 years, to address new governance, management, policy, and infrastructure requirements. This investment comes on top of more than a century of collective investment and efforts to manage the resources of the basin sustainably.

The additional investment and effort have been built on a sound and continually improving knowledge base that has served to inform policy makers of the required response at the basin and the subbasin or catchment levels. Without that knowledge base, decisions of this magnitude could not have been made.

This case study illustrates the need for sound science and for new and more responsive governance at the subnational level; for additional investment; and for integration of adaptation into existing initiatives. It highlights the interrelationships between different levels of government and the community, in the management of all natural resources, and between sound science and policy, governance,

(continued)

BOX 1. Adaptation and River Basin Management: A Case Study (*continued*)

and regulation, as well as related issues such as the need to provide for structural adjustment and the relevance of land-use planning—all in the context of adapting to a changing climate. In the MDB example, strong institutional capacity already existed, and new measures are being built on a sound foundation. The case reinforces the importance of continuing to build core capacity and to plan ahead, especially in generating the capacity to collect and analyze data so that informed choices can be made on the strength of sound science.

Other river basin communities must address their own adaptation issues. The challenge will be greatest where the knowledge base and existing capacity are limited and do not provide a solid foundation on which to build or to make informed decisions.

Building capacity to respond to the impacts of climate change cannot be looked at in isolation from the broader need to build capacity to manage freshwater resources. Increased investments in adaptation provide the opportunity to build more enduring capacity to manage freshwater and other natural resources, which, in turn, will prompt positive spillover effects on areas such as food production and infrastructure.

The scale of change will also require the development and dissemination of improved technologies. Although solutions should be founded on local conditions, policy making and technological developments will also need to be informed by sound science. Finally, none of the suggested solutions can be facilitated without additional investment.

In light of the current and expected impacts of climate change on water resources and their management, and the importance of water for other sectors of the economy and society, governments should recognize that investments in the water sector will not only benefit current generations but will also guarantee sustainable development in the future.

Notes

1. Water-stressed basins are defined as those with per capita water availability of less than 1,000 cubic meters per year.
2. Peaks in population growth are projected to be reached in 2050, at 8.7 billion, in an increasingly globalized world, or in 2100, at 10.4 billion or 15 billion, in a less globalized world (IPCC 2008, 9). A billion is 1,000 million.
3. Governments at the 2002 World Summit on Sustainable Development agreed to develop water management plans on the IWRM principle by 2005, and the concept was endorsed by governments at the 16th session of the United Nations Commission on Sustainable Development in 2008.

References

CCCD (Commission on Climate Change and Development). 2009a. Closing the Gaps: Disaster Risk Reduction and Adaptation to Climate Change in Developing Countries. Stockholm: CCCD. http://www.ccdcommission.org/Filer/report/CCD_REPORT.pdf.

———. 2009b. *The Human Dimension of Climate Adaptation: The Importance of Local and Institutional Issues*. Stockholm: CCCD. http://www.ccdcommission.org/Filer/the_human_dimension_of_climate_adaptation.pdf.

ClimateWorks Foundation. 2009. "Adaptation to Climate Change: Potential Costs and Choice for a Global Agreement. Project Catalyst." ClimateWorks Foundation, San Francisco, CA. http://www.project-catalyst.info/Publications/Working%20Group%20papers/Adaptation%20Potential%20Costsand%20Choices%20for%20a%20Global%20Deal_27%20Mar%2009.pdf.

GWP (Global Water Partnership). 2007. "Climate Change Adaptation and Integrated Water Resource Management—An Initial Overview." Policy Brief 5, Global Water Partnership Secretariat, Stockholm. http://www.gwpforum.org/gwp/library/Policy%20Brief%205%20Climate%20Change%20Adaptation.pdf.

———. 2008. "Perspectives on Water and Climate Change Adaptation: Better Water Resources Management—Greater Resilience Today, More Effective Adaptation Tomorrow." Global Water Partnership Secretariat, Stockholm. http://www.gwpforum.org/gwp/library/Planning_Better_WRM.pdf.

IPCC (Intergovernmental Panel on Climate Change). 2007. "Climate Change 2007: Synthesis Report. Summary for Policymakers." IPCC, Geneva. http://www.ipcc.ch/pdf/assessment-report/ar4/syr/ar4_syr_spm.pdf.

———. 2008. *Climate Change and Water*, ed. Bryson C. Bates, Zbigniew W. Kundzewicz, Shaohong Wu, and Jean Palutikof. Technical Paper VI. Geneva: IPCC. http://www.ipcc.ch/publications_and_data/publications_and_data_technical_papers_climate_change_and_water.htm.

OECD (Organisation for Economic Co-operation and Development) DAC (Development Assistance Committee). 2009. "Issues Paper for High-Level Meeting on Multilateral Aid Effectiveness, Copenhagen, February 2009." OECD, Paris.

Plummer, Janelle, and Tom Slaymaker. 2007. "Rethinking Governance in Water Services." ODI Working Paper 284, Overseas Development Institute, London. http://www.odi.org.uk/resources/download/431.pdf.

Stern, Nicholas. 2007. *The Economics of Climate Change: The Stern Review*. Cambridge, U.K.: Cambridge University Press.

Tearfund. 2008. "Separate Streams? Adapting Water Resources Management to Climate Change." Teddington, U.K. http://www.tearfund.org/webdocs/Website/Campaigning/WATSAN/Separate_streams_web.pdf.

UNFCCC (United Nations Framework Convention on Climate Change). 2007. "Climate Change: Impacts, Vulnerabilities and Adaptation in Developing Countries." UNFCCC Secretariat, Bonn, Germany. http://unfccc.int/resource/docs/publications/ impacts.pdf.

———. 2008. "Investment and Financial Flows to Address Climate Change: An Update." Technical Paper, UNFCCC Secretariat, Bonn, Germany. http://unfccc.int/resource/docs/2008/tp/07.pdf.

WWAP (World Water Assessment Programme). 2009. *The United Nations World Water Development Report 3: Water in a Changing World*. Paris: United Nations Educational, Scientific, and Cultural Organization (UNESCO); London: Earthscan.

The Politics of Climate Policy in Developed Countries

HUGH COMPSTON AND IAN BAILEY

This paper reports the results of a study of the politics of climate policy, in affluent democracies and at the European Union level, aimed at identifying political strategies that may enable governments to make major cuts in greenhouse gas emissions without sustaining significant political damage. Although the focus is on developed countries, many of the findings are relevant to developing countries.

Six major obstacles to the implementation of more radical climate policies are identified: the perception that actions by individual countries make little difference; the continued influence of climate skeptics; a shortage of technically and economically efficacious solutions; the problem of competitiveness; fear of the electorate; and obstacles within government. The main political strategies currently being used to strengthen climate policy in the countries studied are examined. Five strategies are then identified that may make it easier for activist governments to move ahead more rapidly in responding to climate change.

All of the identified obstacles apply to developing as well as developed countries, and the former are additionally hampered by lack of resources. The political strategies identified are also relevant to developing countries, but in some countries the extent of political polarization may make agreement on climate policies difficult, if not impossible.

This paper reports the results of a study of the politics of climate policy in affluent democracies and at the European Union (EU) level. The aim of the study was to identify political strategies that make it easier for governments to cut greenhouse gas emissions substantially without sustaining significant political damage.

Hugh Compston is a reader in politics at Cardiff University, U.K. Ian Bailey is a reader in human geography at the University of Plymouth, U.K.

Berlin Workshop Series 2010
© 2010 The International Bank for Reconstruction and Development / The World Bank

The study, published as *Turning Down the Heat: The Politics of Climate Policy in Affluent Democracies* (Compston and Bailey 2008), is based on three premises:

First, developed countries are not currently implementing the types of policies that need to be carried out if climate change is to be brought under control.

Second, the main reasons for this failing are not scientific, technological, or even economic, but political. Climate science is well established; the Intergovernmental Panel on Climate Change (IPCC) has made increasingly clear statements about the scale, impacts, and origins of recent climate change; and in documents such as the Stern Review (Stern 2007), economists have outlined a range of policy instruments that have the potential to produce major reductions in greenhouse gas emissions without prohibitive economic costs. But still, governments and other political authorities are reluctant to take decisive action, even though most are now convinced that strong measures are needed.

Third, although politicians, officials, and others involved in decision making are in many ways the best placed to understand the constraints and opportunities that exist in national climate politics, political scientists also have a contribution to make because of their different and complementary approaches to the conceptualization and analysis of the dynamics of politics and policy making.

The study provides readers with an overview of the politics of climate policy in the EU and the United States; in five individual EU member states (France, Germany, Greece, Sweden, and the United Kingdom); in Australia and Canada; and in the United States at the state level. Affluent democracies are the focus because these are the countries that have contributed most to current greenhouse gas concentrations and that continue, for the present at least, to be the world's largest emitters, especially in per capita terms. They also tend to be the countries where mitigation capacity, as gauged by technological and financial resources, is furthest advanced. The study focuses mainly on the national and (in federal countries) state levels because that is where most substantive policy measures are formulated and implemented and because the international dimension of climate politics is already well covered in the international relations literature.

The relevance of this study for developing countries is twofold. First, better understanding of the political opportunities and constraints facing developed countries in relation to climate policy should help developing countries deal with developed countries on this issue on a realistic basis. Second, to a considerable extent these same constraints and opportunities also confront the governments of developing countries. A similar study of developing countries is well overdue, but in its absence the results of this analysis are directly relevant.

The academic contributors to the study were asked not only to give an overview of the politics of climate policy but also to identify the main political obstacles to more radical action on climate change, the main political strategies currently being used by governments that want to take action on climate change, and future strategies that might enable these governments to go further without risking disaster at the next election. We look at each of these topics in turn.

Political Obstacles

The contributors identified six major obstacles to the implementation of more radical climate policies.

First obstacle: The perception that individual countries make little difference
It is widely accepted that, with the possible exceptions of the United States and China, unilateral action by any one country to cut its greenhouse gas emissions, however radically, would not even significantly slow global climate change. The absence of a simple cause-and-effect relationship between problem and solution that can be used to justify and legitimate strong climate policies within the domestic political setting is undeniably demotivating for national politicians.

Second obstacle: The influence of climate skeptics
Well-financed climate change skeptics continue to work to undermine support for climate policies by questioning the scientific consensus that climate change is being caused by human actions or by disputing the economic arguments favoring strong action. Where governments are sympathetic to such views, as was the case until recently in the United States, these groups can be a powerful brake on climate policy. The continued accretion of scientific evidence on climate trends and their causes and origins appears to be weakening the ability of climate contrarians to impede the strengthening of climate policies, but their remaining influence has been amplified and prolonged by the media practice of trying to enhance the news value of climate change by framing it as a debate in which the media have a duty to seek "balanced" coverage.

Third obstacle: A shortage of technically and economically efficacious solutions
Despite much hyperbole, potential technological fixes such as hydrogen power, nuclear fusion, and carbon capture and storage are, from a technical or economic point of view, not yet ready to be implemented on a large enough scale to make a difference to climate change.

Fourth obstacle: The problem of competitiveness
Certain climate policy instruments, such as carbon and energy taxes, have the potential to increase production costs for affected firms. To the extent that these firms export goods or compete with imports and foreign firms are not subjected to the same costs, these policies could lead to a loss of international competitiveness that, if serious enough, would result in insolvencies, cutbacks in investments, disinvestment, and, as a consequence, lower economic growth (or recession) and higher unemployment. If affected industries relocate in significant numbers to countries without emissions constraints, overall industry emissions may not be reduced and may even increase ("carbon leakage"). Industry groups and associated concerns are rarely slow to bring these potential effects to the attention of politicians and officials. It is, therefore, not surprising that market-based instruments that are thought to erode competitiveness have often been avoided or diluted through the introduction of exemptions and concessions for energy-intensive or trade-exposed firms. Fears about losses in competitiveness have also contributed to member state resistance to the tightening of emissions caps under the EU emissions trading scheme.

The obvious response to this problem is to level the playing field for domestic and foreign firms. Although there is little immediate prospect of this happening at the global level, in 2008 the European Commission flirted with the concept of compensating for the increased costs incurred by European firms by imposing a carbon import tariff. More ambitiously, the introduction of a common carbon tax across all EU countries would prevent competitive distortions within the Single European Market, although this would not help European-based companies vis-à-vis firms based outside the EU. Some member states, however, remain opposed to ceding any further taxation powers to the EU.

Fifth obstacle: Fear of the electorate
Growing public sympathy for the general notion of climate protection is arguably a major factor behind the emergence in many countries of greater cross-party agreement on the need for stronger climate policies. Individuals, however, tend to be less supportive of climate policies that directly or indirectly impose personal costs or that impinge in other ways on personal freedoms, such as carbon and energy taxes and restrictions on vehicle use. Employees whose jobs are perceived to be threatened by measures such as carbon taxes are also likely to object. Democratic governments which ignore these objections risk losing votes in the next general election that may make the difference between retaining and losing office. Where parties are polarized on particular climate policies, there is the further risk that an activist government would lose office to parties that have gained votes by promising to reverse these policies, so that even a noble sacrifice would be in vain.

Sixth obstacle: Obstacles within government
Control of the executive in countries such as the United Kingdom generally ensures safe passage through the parliamentary system for the government's preferred policies. By contrast, in countries such as the United States, legislatures can and do regularly block government proposals. In federal countries, subnational governments possess constitutional powers that, depending on their specificity, enable them either to interfere with the implementation of the central government's preferred policies or to set independent agendas for climate policy. Another obstacle within government is the tendency of economic and energy ministries to oppose climate policies that are thought to have negative economic effects. The ability of such ministries to block or dilute climate policies is enhanced by the fact that responsibility for critical areas such as energy and transport is generally located in economic rather than environmental ministries. Although the opposition of economically oriented ministries is not necessarily enough to block climate policies if heads of government are determined to pursue them, lack of effective leadership at the top is often an obstacle to greater progress on climate change.

Current Strategies

The contributors identify a number of typical political strategies that are currently being used by governments in developed countries to strengthen climate policy.

Efforts to reach global agreement on climate change
Governments continue driving for global agreements that deepen the commitments made by developed countries to cut emissions and that broaden the range of countries entering into binding commitments—for example, by promising financial assistance and technology transfer for developing countries if they agree.

Reports and targets
Government reporting and target setting can, in some cases, be used as substitutes for action. When not used cynically, however, reports and targets can play an important role in diagnosing the scale of the problem, specifying required outcomes, and, in so doing, providing a statement of intent, building support for action, and informing the structure and design of policy instruments. That said, a recurrent finding is that targets are often missed.

A focus on climate policies on which all major relevant political actors can agree
One way in which governments can limit the political damage associated with climate policies is to obtain the prior agreement of the main affected political actors and, implicitly, of the electorate, as indicated by the results of opinion polls. This approach has pervaded the climate politics of many of the case study countries. One indication of its use is the ubiquity of voluntary agreements whereby industry groups undertake to reduce their emissions in exchange for the nonimposition or delay of legal requirements or economic instruments. Although instances exist of climate policies being imposed by governments over political opposition—an example is the German ecotax of the late 1990s—in general, this has occurred only after lengthy debates or periods of reliance on voluntary commitments, and the imposition of such policies has often been accompanied by concessionary measures.

The experience of affluent democracies demonstrates that a wide range of climate policies exists on which broad agreement can be reached. Consensus strategies are particularly important in the early stages of climate policy as a means of binding key actors (especially industry groups) to the principle of emissions reduction while avoiding excessive political costs. But once the policies on which agreement can be reached have been implemented, persistence in a consensus strategy can impede further progress because of the effective veto that the perceived need for agreement gives relevant stakeholders.

Incrementalism on many fronts
One widely shared belief among policy analysts and practitioners is that incremental policy changes usually elicit less political opposition than radical policy changes and can create a platform for more ambitious policy changes. It is, therefore, not surprising that most governments in affluent democracies have tended to implement a wide variety of relatively weak policies rather than adopt a few big, radical measures. The emissions trading schemes introduced in the EU and some U.S. states do, however, constitute major departures from past practices.

Taking advantage of weather-related natural disasters to heighten awareness of climate risks

Even though it is impossible to be certain that individual weather-related disasters are a direct result of climate change, scientific research linking extreme weather events to climate change has fueled media speculation on the subject when such events occur. The resulting spikes in public concern about climate change create windows of opportunity for governments to introduce or strengthen climate policies without sustaining as much political damage as might ensue at other·times. It is important to note that these windows of opportunity tend to close as the event becomes more distant in time and the media move on to other issues. There is evidence that, in some cases, governments have grasped these opportunities, as happened in Germany in 2002, when the Elbe floods were instrumental in the government's introduction of new targets.

Framing climate policy as contributing to other policy objectives

An increasingly common device used by governments to broaden support for particular climate policies is to stress their contribution to the achievement of other social and economic objectives (so-called ancillary benefits and cobenefits). Expansion of energy generation from renewable sources, for example, contributes to energy security and employment, as well as to climate change mitigation, while measures to encourage people to switch from private cars to public transport would be expected to reduce traffic congestion as well as greenhouse gas emissions. The advantage of this approach is that actors who support these other objectives can be recruited to swell advocacy coalitions favoring, directly or indirectly, the objectives of climate policy.

Choosing appropriate policy instruments

In general, governments have moved from relying on voluntary agreements toward using economic instruments underpinned by legal requirements. Among the most commonly used instruments are

- Information provision
- Encouragement of new technologies through subsidies and grants
- Encouragement of renewable energy production by obliging electricity utilities either to provide a certain proportion of electricity from renewable sources (quotas) or to buy all electricity produced by renewable sources at a set price (feed-in tariff)
- Regulation to enforce improvements in energy efficiency
- Emissions trading
- Carbon and energy taxes.

Important considerations in the choice and design of instruments have included effectiveness in reducing emissions in the targeted sector, legal enforceability, ease of monitoring, safeguarding of reasonable equity and protection of vulnerable or politically powerful groups, and control of the impacts of the policy instrument on international competitiveness.

Looking to the Future

The evidence provided by the contributors led to the identification of a number of strategies that should make it easier for governments to go further on climate change without sustaining significant political damage.

Refinement of current strategies
The most obvious strategy is for governments to continue to further develop the political strategies already being used. This can be done by

- Redoubling efforts to strengthen global agreements in a way that also promotes greater involvement by developing nations
- Improving reporting of climate change trends and predictions
- Improving communication of the policy instruments that are needed and the benefits they will produce
- Introducing progressively stricter emissions and policy targets
- Identifying and implementing further policies on which all powerful actors can agree
- Preparing measures that can be implemented swiftly in response to weather-related natural disasters and other events that heighten public concern about climate change
- Continuing to stress the contribution of climate policies to other policy objectives such as energy security
- Incrementally strengthening existing policies, especially economic instruments and financial incentives that promote technological innovation and renewable energy.

Exploration of new policy options
The second strategy is for governments to introduce policies such as

- Much more stringent energy-efficiency regulations
- Much bigger financial incentives for energy-efficiency improvements
- *Grand projet*–style investments in new infrastructure, such as massive new investment in nuclear power, to create stepwise reductions in emissions
- Extension of emissions trading to the individual level through the introduction of tradable personal carbon allowances
- Introduction of carbon import tariffs at the EU level to compensate for any losses in international competitiveness caused by the adoption of stringent climate policies.

Governance reform
A third strategy is to reform the way in which climate policy is governed by

- Improving the measurement of emissions (to enhance the credibility of emissions data)
- Devoting more resources to systematic envisioning of what a low-carbon society would look like, in order to make it easier to identify the policies needed to get there
- Improving the integration of economic and environmental governance by measures such as moving energy and transport into an environmental ministry

- Creating a separate climate ministry in order to raise the political profile of climate policy
- Providing seats for independent experts and environmental nongovernmental organizations on all official climate change–related committees on which industry is represented
- Ensuring that able and committed individuals are placed in key posts
- Improving the transparency of potentially popular initiatives
- Distributing any costs imposed by climate policies more equitably, on the premise that initiatives are more likely to be acceptable if they are perceived as being fair.

Spillover strategies

"Spillover policies" are policies that are relatively easy to transfer to other countries, difficult to reverse once introduced, or effective in creating functional or political pressure for their own strengthening or for the introduction of related measures. Examples are policies that lead to greater investment and employment in the renewables sector and thus increase pressures exerted by employers and unions for governments to facilitate further expansion of the sector. The aim of a spillover strategy is to select and implement policies that (a) increase the pressure on other governments to implement similar policies and (b) increase pressure for stronger policies to be applied at home.

Selective imposition of more radical policies

By focusing on measures on which the agreement of powerful actors can be obtained, governments have been able to introduce and strengthen a number of climate policies at relatively low political cost. Once these relatively uncontroversial policies have been negotiated and implemented, however, the continued assumption that broad agreement has to be obtained impedes the introduction of more radical measures by giving all stakeholders an effective veto on government action. This, combined with the fact that consensus strategies have not (yet) delivered emissions cuts of the magnitude required to mitigate climate change effectively, suggests that governments that are serious about significantly reducing emissions will at some point need to impose more radical policies against the wishes of powerful actors or voters—that is, to adopt a strategy of selective policy imposition. Such an approach clearly carries greater political risks than consensus strategies, but certain tactics can limit the risks. Governments can

- Introduce unpopular policies during the early years of an administration to allow time for opposition to subside and for the benefits of the policies to become apparent before the next election arrives.
- Target economic sectors that are able to pass on at least a proportion of their extra costs to consumers. This approach may facilitate the internalization of environmental costs without the government being blamed directly (although the media are often quick to publicize how carbon and energy taxes, for example, lead to higher prices for consumers).
- Adopt policies that target losses on small sections of society, particularly groups that are least able to inflict political damage via the ballot box or to exercise threats to withdraw investment from the country.

- Compensate powerful actors in order to weaken their resistance to more progressive climate policies, although this approach is open to accusations of unfairness and inequity if the groups in question are responsible for large quantities of greenhouse gas emissions. In order to limit political damage, such compensation measures would need to be accompanied by a clear message that compensation is contingent on action and greater cooperation with the objectives of climate policy.

Conclusion

The foregoing is by no means a definitive picture of the politics of climate policy even in developed countries, let alone developing countries. It does, however, provide a fairly comprehensive overview that is, at the same time, forward looking in that it aids thinking about what might help governments do what is needed while minimizing political damage.

It is also surprisingly relevant to developing countries. Developing countries confront all the political obstacles facing the governments of developed countries, plus the additional burden of lack of resources. Even authoritarian regimes need to be sensitive to public opinion—although the absence of elections might enable them to move more swiftly than a democratic government could. All the political strategies currently being used by the governments of developed countries could be employed by their developing counterparts, although in some countries the extent of political polarization may make any sort of agreement on climate policies difficult, if not impossible, and lack of resources limits the use of costly policy instruments such as subsidies. Finally, in broad terms, the new political strategies identified are also relevant to developing countries, although lack of resources is, again, a serious constraint, and in at least some cases improving governance may be of special relevance.

References

Compston, Hugh, and Ian Bailey, eds. 2008. *Turning Down the Heat: The Politics of Climate Policy in Affluent Democracies.* Houndmills, Basingstoke, Hampshire, U.K.: Palgrave Macmillan.

Stern, Nicholas. 2007. *The Economics of Climate Change: The Stern Review.* Cambridge, U.K.: Cambridge University Press.